Equatorial Guinea

WORLD BIBLIOGRAPHICAL SERIES

General Editors:
Robert G. Neville (Executive Editor)
John J. Horton

Robert A. Myers   Ian Wallace
Hans H. Wellisch   Ralph Lee Woodward, Jr.

John J. Horton is Deputy Librarian of the University of Bradford and currently Chairman of its Academic Board of Studies in Social Sciences. He has maintained a longstanding interest in the discipline of area studies and its associated bibliographical problems, with special reference to European Studies. In particular he has published in the field of Icelandic and of Yugoslav studies, including the two relevant volumes in the World Bibliographical Series.

Robert A. Myers is Associate Professor of Anthropology in the Division of Social Sciences and Director of Study Abroad Programs at Alfred University, Alfred, New York. He has studied post-colonial island nations of the Caribbean and has spent two years in Nigeria on a Fulbright Lectureship. His interests include international public health, historical anthropology and developing societies. In addition to *Amerindians of the Lesser Antilles: a bibliography* (1981), *A Resource Guide to Dominica, 1493–1986* (1987) and numerous articles, he has compiled the World Bibliographical Series volumes on *Dominica* (1987), *Nigeria* (1989) and *Ghana* (1991).

Ian Wallace is Professor of German at the University of Bath. A graduate of Oxford in French and German, he also studied in Tübingen, Heidelberg and Lausanne before taking teaching posts at universities in the USA, Scotland and England. He specializes in contemporary German affairs, especially literature and culture, on which he has published numerous articles and books. In 1979 he founded the journal *GDR Monitor*, which he continues to edit under its new title *German Monitor*.

Hans H. Wellisch is Professor emeritus at the College of Library and Information Services, University of Maryland. He was President of the American Society of Indexers and was a member of the International Federation for Documentation. He is the author of numerous articles and several books on indexing and abstracting, and has published *The Conversion of Scripts* and *Indexing and Abstracting: an International Bibliography*. He also contributes frequently to *Journal of the American Society for Information Science, The Indexer* and other professional journals.

Ralph Lee Woodward, Jr. is Chairman of the Department of History at Tulane University, New Orleans, where he has been Professor of History since 1970. He is the author of *Central America, a Nation Divided*, 2nd ed. (1985), as well as several monographs and more than sixty scholarly articles on modern Latin America. He has also compiled volumes in the World Bibliographical Series on *Belize* (1980), *Nicaragua* (1983), and *El Salvador* (1988). Dr. Woodward edited the Central American section of the *Research Guide to Central America and the Caribbean* (1985) and is currently editor of the Central American history section of the *Handbook of Latin American Studies*.

VOLUME 136

Equatorial Guinea

Randall Fegley

Compiler

CLIO PRESS

OXFORD, ENGLAND · SANTA BARBARA, CALIFORNIA
DENVER, COLORADO

British Library Cataloguing in Publication Data

Fegley, Randall
Equatorial Guinea – (World Bibliographical Series)
I. Title   II. Series
016.9671803

ISBN 1–85109–167–X

Clio Press Ltd.,
55 St. Thomas' Street,
Oxford OX1 1JG, England.

ABC-CLIO,
130 Cremona Drive,
Santa Barbara,
CA 93117, USA.

Designed by Bernard Crossland.
Typeset by Columns Design and Production Services Ltd., Reading, England.
Printed and bound in Great Britain by
Billing and Sons Ltd., Worcester.

THE WORLD BIBLIOGRAPHICAL SERIES

This series, which is principally designed for the English speaker, will eventually cover every country (and many of the world's principal regions), each in a separate volume comprising annotated entries on works dealing with its history, geography, economy and politics; and with its people, their culture, customs, religion and social organization. Attention will also be paid to current living conditions – housing, education, newspapers, clothing, etc.– that are all too often ignored in standard bibliographies; and to those particular aspects relevant to individual countries. Each volume seeks to achieve, by use of careful selectivity and critical assessment of the literature, an expression of the country and an appreciation of its nature and national aspirations, to guide the reader towards an understanding of its importance. The keynote of the series is to provide, in a uniform format, an interpretation of each country that will express its culture, its place in the world, and the qualities and background that make it unique. The views expressed in individual volumes, however, are not necessarily those of the publisher.

VOLUMES IN THE SERIES

Contents

Contents

Preface

Equatorial Guinea is one of the least known countries in the world. Those seeking information on the country are faced with numerous limitations. Relatively little has been written on Equatorial Guinea in English (apart from works written in a brief period of British influence in the second half of the 19th century and works on dictatorship and human rights written since the mid-1970s). Since independence the nature of the country's politics has led to isolation from the world press, numerous restrictions on information, questionable facts and figures and the destruction of records. Hence much material on the country is dated, though not necessarily obsolete. The number of sources is also restricting. In writing a bibliography of Equatorial Guinea, I found a sizeable body of works from a very few authors (Panyella-Gómez, Nosti Nava, Bravo Carbonell, Pélissier, Fernandez, Sundiata, Volio Jimenez as well as the world's foremost expert on Equatorial Guinea, Max Liniger-Goumaz). Very few works (apart from technical and scientific ones) do not have marked political biases. The majority of printed sources on Equatorial Guinea come from one institution, the Instituto de Estudios Africanos in Madrid (or its division the Consejo Superior de Investigaciones Científicas – Higher Council of Scientific Investigation). Although this centre has produced some excellent material on the country, much of its work has Falangist, racist and/or colonialist prejudices. Similarly, since independence, a good deal of material has been produced by businesses, human rights organizations, left-wing groups and governments. These sources also carry sometimes severe biases. Perhaps with no other country does the issue of truth and falsehood weigh so heavily on the reader and researcher. One must also note that any extensive study of Equatorial Guinea is likely to involve large numbers of official documents and technical studies, some of which are rare and many of which are not readily available in the anglophone world.

The general aim of this bibliography is to present Equatorial Guinea in all its facets to the English-speaking world. Entries have been selected for their authority, variety, and ease of access. Priority has been given to works in English, but the lack of English-language sources on whole aspects of Equatorial Guinean life has meant that large amounts of Spanish and French material are also required. The citation order within each section is alphabetical by author. Items are annotated to provide a summary of each work's contents, author, significance and viewpoint, and an index of authors, titles and subjects is also included.

I am indebted to many people for assistance not only in the completion of this book, but also in their continuing encouragement of my work on Equatorial Guinea. They include Professor C. M. Eya Nchama who has shown much interest and assisted in numerous ways; Professor Max Liniger-Goumaz who has also given a good deal of his time over the years; and others whose information and opinions filled in the picture. I would like to thank the library staff members at Howard University and Pennsylvania State University for their patient assistance. But, as always, my deepest appreciation goes to my wife, Connie.

Randall Fegley
Reading, Pennsylvania
August 1991

Introduction

The Republic of Equatorial Guinea consists of two islands, Fernando Po (also known as Bioko) and Annobón, in the Gulf of Guinea and Río Muni, an enclave wedged between Gabon and Cameroon.

With a coastline of 250 kilometres and an area of 2,017 square miles, Fernando Po consists of several extinct volcanoes. The highest, Pico de Santa Isabel, is 3,007 metres high and provides an excellent view of the Nigerian and Cameroonian coasts, one of the most strategically important stretches of the African coast. A second volcano, Moka, has a crater lake at 1,800 metres, giving it an uncanny appearance which has caught the eye of many a traveller. In this century Moka has proved to be the only feasible livestock-breeding area in the tsetse fly-ravaged Gulf of Guinea. A third volcano is a broken-down crater rim which provides a deep-water harbour on the northern end of the island. The shoreline is rugged with only occasional beaches and coves.

Annobón is a wind-swept Atlantic island of only seven square miles.

Río Muni is a rectangular enclave with an area of 9,459 square miles. Behind a narrow coastal plain rise hills with some of the densest forests on the continent. Although the soil is only mediocre, high rainfall, temperatures and humidity have produced lush vegetation which includes some 140 species of trees. Animal and bird life is extremely varied though not very great in numbers. Most of the enclave drains into the Río Benito, which runs through the territory from east to west. The Río Campo forms the northern border and the Muni Estuary in the south has areas of almost impenetrable mangrove forest.

Introduction

Ethnic groups

The island peoples consist of the indigenous Bubis; the Fernandinos who are the descendants of freed slaves; and the now dwindled Nigerian plantation workforce.

Because of the variety of anthropological types and the presence of four dialects among the Bubi, it is more than likely the tribe is a composite group formed from mainland groups who arrived at different times. At Playa Carboneras on Fernando Po, three distinct earlier cultures have been unearthed by archaeologists. They also may have contributed to the group. The Bubi have been monotheistic, monogamous and matrilineal as far back as their history has been recorded. Although their origins may have been fragmentary, the Bubi established a kingdom with priests, local chiefs and a king. Bubi currency consisted of rounded pieces of shell, still used for jewellery. The island's early society was divided according to occupation. Traditionally, the Bubis were not interested in trade and had little desire to maintain contacts with the outside world. At various points in their history they retreated to Moka Mountain which is regarded as sacred. Until well into this century, hostility and isolation were hallmarks of the tribe. The Bubis were originally farmers, but gradually their farms were amalgamated by the colonial plantations. Both the Bubis and the Fernandinos were converted to Christianity by missionaries and became Hispanicized.

Along Río Muni's coastal plain and river estuaries are the Ndowe. Collectively, this group is often called *Los Playeros* (the Beach People), but this name is misleading because some Ndowe groups extend well inland and the entire group is believed to have originated in the African interior. In the strictest sense, the Ndowe are those tribes which speak Kombe (the Kombe, Bomoundi, Asangon, Minko, and others), but in a wider sense they also include the Benga, Balenke, Bujeba and even the Bayele pygmies.

The majority of the people of Río Muni are Fang. The Fang were traditionally hunters and subsistence farmers. Unlike the island groups, they never fully accepted Christianity and remained outside the colonial system. This tribe, known first as the *Pahouin*, was mistakenly believed to be nomadic. Having suffered environmental dislocation farther north, they migrated into the jungles. Their entry into their present tribal area, which extends into Cameroon and Gabon, occurred from about 1820 to 1890 and coincided with European settlement on the adjacent coast.

The Fang were feared largely because a myth of cannibalism had developed around them. In fact they were never cannibal in the sense that human beings were part of their diet, but their early witchcraft societies practised necrophagy or the eating of parts of unburied corpses to assimilate qualities of the deceased. Over the years these practices died out. The human sacrifices of the later Bwiti cult had no necrophaganous element at all and the skulls found in Fang houses to this day are not the results of cannibalism, but are the icons of an ancestor-worshipping culture.

The social structure of the Fang is exceedingly complex. They are polygynous and patrilinear, with authority vested in head men and sorcerers. In the northern sectors of the Fang area there are clear subdivisions, but southern Fang groups are fragmented and interspersed. In Río Muni the tribe is divided into Ntumu (northern) and Okak (southern) branches with the Río Benito being the boundary between the two. In order to strengthen intergroup relations and prevent incest, double exogamy is practised. This promoted the geographical extension of kinship ties and with them, trade. Sexual morality is highly valued and is thought to be a prerequisite for the divine granting of fertility. This is reinforced by the region's very low fertility rate: Gabon has the lowest in Africa and Río Muni the second lowest.

The long prelude to colonization

In the early 1470s, Portuguese seafarers made their way around west Africa as part of the effort to evade the Venetian-Ottoman monopoly on trade with the East. In the course of a number of voyages, they discovered four volcanic islands. Though uninhabited, the southernmost, later named Annobón, was to serve the Portuguese Empire as a foothold in Africa. Northeast were two larger islands which were also uninhabited: Sïo Tomé and Principe. Finally, a still larger island was found northeast of these. The Portuguese called it 'Formosa' ('the Beautiful'). Green with forests, 'Formosa' officially became known as Fernando Po (or Fernando Póo), supposedly a corruption of Fernïo de Poo, a Portuguese captain's name. These four islands along with Mount Cameroon and the Adamawa Range on the African mainland form a chain of volcanos.

The Portuguese noted both the economic and strategic potential of Fernando Po. The island's volcanic soils and sloping mountains allowed the cultivation of almost anything. Cinchona, oil palms and sugar-cane grew wild. Up to 800 metres in height the island was covered with forests and only occasionally broken by villages; between 1,200 and 1,500 metres, meadowlands and groves of tree-ferns dominate. The Gulf of Guinea was rich in fish and other sea-life.

Rich though it may have been, Fernando Po was not some sort of paradise. The islands and adjacent coast have an extremely wet climate with oppressive humidity. Although the highlands are cooler, extremes of temperature encourage illnesses of all sorts. By 1500 the first traders were established on Annobón, the healthiest island. With the Europeans came the slave trade. Sïo Tomé and Principe were settled by the Portuguese, but Annobón and Fernando Po remained sparsely settled, the former because of size and the latter due to a variety of difficulties. These included disease, the Bubis' hold on the land and the technological limitations of the day which precluded the clearing of dense mountain vegetation under tropical conditions. In spite of these obstacles, the Portuguese were able to introduce two activities which were to have profound effects on the island: coffee cultivation and the slave trade. As a result of the latter, the Bubis spent much of the next 400 years avoiding contact with all Europeans.

On 1 October 1777 Spain and Portugal signed the Treaty of San Ildefonso which granted Portugal some minor Spanish territories adjacent to Brazil and gave Spain territories and rights which included Fernando Po, Annobón and a section of the West African coast. Six months later, the Treaty of El Pardo, reaffirmed Spanish sovereignty over the two islands and determined that Spain's coastal rights extended from the Niger to the Ogoowe. Shortly after the signing of the El Pardo treaty, a Spanish expedition under Brigadier Felipe José, Count of Argelejos de Santos y Freire was dispatched from Uruguay to take possession of the new colonies. Arriving at Fernando Po in October 1778, Argelejos claimed the island for the Spanish king. The expedition then left for Annobón, but on the way Argelejos died and the fever-ridden crew mutinied and imprisoned the Count's lieutenant. The expedition was forced to land on Sïo Tomé and the Portuguese authorities there arrested the crew. After further bouts of illness, the expedition limped back into Montevideo in February 1783. The sight of an unsuccessful expedition returning with a crew in irons and 124 of its 150 men not returning at all proved too much for the Spanish. As a result of this five-year fiasco, Madrid took almost no interest in tropical Africa for half a century. Quite apart from the hazards involved, the far-flung Spanish Empire was rapidly coming to an end. In the first half of the 19th century, revolutionary insurrection was rife in Spain's American colonies from Cape Horn to Texas. Until the late 1840s Madrid could not afford to turn her attentions and dwindling finances from the Western Hemisphere. With the decline of the slave trade and the rise of other forms of commerce came the occupation of vast tracts of Africa by Europeans, a strategy which the cautious Spanish court was both unwilling and unable to pursue.

For several years the British had been trying to supplant the Spanish in Fernando Po. In 1821 a Captain Kelly landed on the eastern shore of Fernando Po. Kelly, who was the first to use the term 'Bubi', found a settlement at Concepción and chose the submerged crater on the northern end of the island as the site for a future base. In 1807 Britain had outlawed slavery and a decade later Spain agreed to abolish the slave trade north of the Equator. A narrow-minded Spanish government felt Fernando Po's *raison d'être* had vanished. Following the failure of a few half-hearted attempts at development, the Spanish leased the island to Great Britain as a forward naval base for anti-slavery patrols. The short period of British administration which followed brought profound changes.

Following the 1817 Anglo-Spanish agreement leasing Fernando Po to Britain, the crater harbour became a *de facto* colony of the Royal Navy. British naval captain and leader of an anti-slavery commission, Fitz-William Owen founded a settlement which was named Port Clarence. Within a few months, three-quarters of the expedition's members had died of various diseases. Port Clarence was known as 'death's waiting room', a nickname which would stay with the settlement for the rest of the century.

John Beecroft, British governor of Clarence from 1833 to 1854, was one of the most interesting characters in the region's history. A mulatto civil servant, he was superintendent of the Owen Expedition. In 1834 the British naval base at Port Clarence was closed down and Beecroft stayed on to administer the settlement. He opened trading posts in Port Clarence and on the Cameroonian coast as agencies of the British company, Dillon and Tenant. Although not lucky in trade, he was by no means a poor man and his career as an administrator and imperialist more than compensated for his business difficulties. The British government created the post of Consul of the Bights of Biafra and Benin in order to protect their growing interests in Nigeria. Beecroft was appointed to this post and, using Fernando Po as a springboard, he began to push Britain's sphere of direct influence up the Niger. His agents occupied Lagos and secured the Nigerian coast for Britain. There had been much discussion of selling the colony to the United Kingdom, but Spain's parliament, the *Cortes*, opposed the sale of any colonies. Moreover, the Spanish public expected to see their country have a presence in Africa. Hence, in 1843, Queen Isabella dispatched a commission headed by Royal Plenipotentiary Juan José de Lerena y Bary to Port Clarence. On arrival, he appointed Beecroft governor without pay. In this capacity, Beecroft introduced customs duties and maintained order on Fernando Po. His twenty-one years on the island are recorded with praise in both London and Madrid. His position as an agent for more than one government was not unique. One needs only to look at the examples of Gordon and Stanley to see that multiple employment of this kind was not exceptional.

After directing that all place-names be changed to Spanish ones, Lerena y Bary set up the colony's first court and ordered Protestant missionaries to depart. Leaving Beecroft in command, he left for the mainland where he signed treaties with several hundred chiefs and granted Spanish nationality to the Ndowe tribes. He then reaffirmed the Spanish claim to Annobón and returned to Spain. Lerena's trip was followed in 1845 by a lightning tour by the Spanish consul in Sierra Leone, Adolfo Guillemar de Aragón who notified French authorities in Gabon that the southern limit of Spanish territory was Cape Santa Clara.

The most lasting effects of British influence on Fernando Po are connected with the settlement of ex-slaves. Slaves rescued by anti-slavery patrols were settled on the island. Later, liberated Angolan slaves, Crioulos (Portuguese-African mulattos), and a large influx of immigrants from Liberia, Sierra Leone and Nigeria arrived. Collectively, these peoples became known as the Fernandinos. Frequently speaking a number of coastal languages, they formed a tightly knit entrepreneurial group and profited as middlemen between the white man and the native residents of the Gulf of Guinea. One arrival was a West Indian freeman, William Pratt. Noting the similarity between Fernando Po's soil and climate and that of the West Indies, he sent off to the Caribbean for cacao seeds. The experimental plantings on his holdings proved successful and eventually a Ghanian, Tetteh Quashie, took the new crop to the mainland in 1879. Within a short time Fernando Po developed into a one-crop plantation economy based on cacao.

Spanish colonialism's beginnings

Spurred on by the worldwide rush for palm oil, the British decided the consulship should be full-time and the Spanish government decided to put their own man in Santa Isabel (the Spanish name for Port Clarence). Thus the dual roles of consul and governor were ended. In May 1858, Carlos Chacón, the first Spanish governor of Fernando Po, arrived with an engineer, a doctor, Jesuits and infantry. In his eight months as governor he was able to lay the groundwork for Spain's future colonization. He proclaimed Catholicism official and expelled Baptist missionaries, who had not obeyed the 1844 orders. Chacón had the access to the harbour improved, built some roads and conducted a census. On the mainland, he levied a toll on boats using the Muni Estuary, an act which infuriated the French.

His replacement, José de la Gandara, arrived with 128 settlers and 166 soldiers, but after ten months, only three settlers and about eighty soldiers remained. Jews, Cuban political prisoners, Spanish colonists from Morocco and Algeria and Catalan traders were brought in. Most died, moved on or escaped the nightmare which Santa Isabel had become.

Many European explorers used Fernando Po as a base; among them were Richard Lemon Lander who is buried just outside Santa Isabel, Sir Richard Francis Burton who was British consul (1861-64), Henry Morton Stanley and others. The most impressive of these was Mary Henrietta Kingsley. Daughter of a highly educated but cruel father and a sickly demanding mother, her childhood was given to dreams of travel, scientific curiosity and the development of an exuberant sense of humour, three characteristics evident in virtually everything she was to write later. After her parents died, she signed on to become a palm oil trader in West Africa. Particularly interested in plants, fish and local customs, she kept in touch with some of Britain's top scholars on Africa, sending them samples, drawings and reports. Mary's books made her both rich and famous.

Kingsley arrived at Santa Isabel in 1893. Many changes had occurred in the town since the first Spanish colonization attempts. Health on the island improved after 1870 when Governor General Zoilo Sanchez Ocaña suggested the island's elevated areas should be used. One year later, Governor General José Montes de Oca established his residence and administration at Basile, south of Santa Isabel at a height of 450 metres. The benefits of higher altitude, which were freely offered to all Europeans, improved the health situation somewhat. In spite of this, Kingsley noted that the appointment of the Spanish governor general was still 'equivalent to execution, only more uncomfortable in the way it worked out'. Earlier, an outbreak of yellow fever had killed 78 of the 280 whites on the island. The thirty-one years which followed the epidemic saw the establishment of many new plantations and the increased use of the highlands, but little change in Santa Isabel. Disease combined with the removal of whites to Basile meant few of the amenities found in ports such as Dakar and Freetown were available. Mary describes Santa Isabel as a 'dilapidated little town', 'sound asleep and its streets weed-grown'. But the town and plantations were expanding and much labour was required. Kru tribesmen were recruited from Liberia on a very dubious basis. They were usually kept for longer periods than they had engaged themselves for, and their conditions were such that returning workers spread tuberculosis and venereal diseases throughout Liberia. Alcoholism was rampant.

In spite of first impressions, Mary warmed to Fernando Po, after getting a chance to study the Bubi who had just emerged from isolation. Delving into past works, particularly those of Oskar Baumann, Mary was able to combine good research with her own experiences in order to detail the Bubis' history and customs. Returning on numerous occasions, she grew attached to the island, and went on to explore the Ogoowe in Gabon where she traded and travelled for a year and a half. A good deal of her research has remained authoritative to this day. Supporting the British cause during the Boer War, she signed on as a nurse and cared for Boer prisoners, but eventually, she contracted enteric fever and died on 3 June 1900. She was buried at sea after an amazing life of only thirty-eight years.

In the last two decades of the 19th century, the British, French and Spanish were all involved in a race for territory on the Gulf of Guinea, but the power running ahead of all these was a newcomer, Germany. In 1849 the Hamburg-based company of Adolf Woermann sent agents to the coast. Kept out of the Niger delta by the British, Woermann's agents opened offices along the coast from Mount Cameroon to southern Gabon, expanding to both the Spanish and Portuguese islands and the inland river valleys by the 1880s. Other German firms followed. These companies sponsored missions and assisted explorers, but the British continued to administer the Nigerian coast from Santa Isabel until 1882 when the office of Consul of the Bights of Biafra and Benin was moved to the mainland in response to German ambitions. The last consul to hold the title was Edward H. Hewett, who has gone down in history as 'Too Late Hewett' because he arrived in Cameroon to sign treaties just as the German flag was being raised. The French did somewhat better than the British in opposing Berlin's challenge: unable to extend too far from their base in Libreville, they still insured German claims south of the Río Campo were invalidated.

The Spanish were the least successful imperial power in equatorial Africa. For years Spain and her colony Cuba had been plagued with unrest. These upheavals were unsuccessful at first, but eventually two monarchs were deposed. Had it not been for a handful of dedicated explorers and traders, it is probable Spain would have been excluded from the continent's mainland entirely. In 1877, Belgian King Leopold II created a Madrid section of his *Association Internationale Africaine*. In reaction to this, the wholly Spanish *Sociedad de Africanistas y Colonialistas* was founded to maximize Spanish claims. Foremost in this new venture was a Basque named Manuel Iradier y Bulfy. He was a self-made man but unlike most of that tough breed of humanity, Iradier's accomplishments were not in business, administration or the military, but in philosophy and art. Yearning for travel, Iradier was able to collect 10,000 pesetas and set out on an expedition in January 1875.

He landed on Corisco Island in the Muni Estuary. This area already had a long history when Iradier arrived. Along the coast and on the nearby islands were several small tribes of the Ndowe group. The Benga of the Muni Estuary were the best organized of these groups. Under a 19th-century dynasty of three kings each named Bonkoro, they saw Christianization and the establishment of a money economy. Although Corisco Island is less than five and a half square miles in area, it has been important ever since the Portuguese used it as a slaving yard. The Benga first arrived on the island in the early 18th century and took up a semi-European lifestyle, as middlemen and guides. In 1815, an American Presbyterian mission had been established on the island, a strange partner for the island's other outpost of white civilization, the slaving base which was destroyed in 1840. Three American Protestant schools with 100 pupils were operating in 1860. Corisco and the nearby Elobeyes Islands became major trading depots. As many as twenty-two ships were anchored in the estuary at a time for just one of the numerous companies. The island, which in 1887 had only 609 inhabitants, was quickly over-run and new sites on the mainland were developed. Along the Río Utamboni, which flows southwest into the estuary, the riverbanks were dotted with the warehouses of British, German, French and Catalan firms. Used by steamers as far as sixty miles upstream, the river became the penetration route of explorers and traders. Among them was Iradier.

After criss-crossing the Muni, surveying the Utamboni and climbing mountains on the way, Iradier settled down in Santa Isabel for a rest. It was January 1876 and, short of money, he took a teaching post. But a *wanderlust* had imbedded itself in the young explorer and soon he was back on the mainland, this time to make a gruelling but thorough tour of the territory which lasted 884 days and covered 1,876 kilometres. Feeling quite justifiably that he had something to tell the Spanish public, he returned to Europe. Like many innovators, Iradier was met with little understanding when he spoke of the opportunities offered in Africa. But the ignorance was not total, and the *Sociedad de Africanistas y Colonialistas* found in Iradier the makings of a Spanish Stanley. With the backing of the society, he set out on a second expedition. Two companions joined the party: José Montes de Oca, later to be governor general of the colony, and Amadeo Ossorio Zabala, a founding member of the society and one of Iradier's financiers. Time had become important: Nachtigal had just completed the occupation of the Cameroon coast for Germany; the United Kingdom had secured its hold on the Niger and Old Calabar; French influence was strong. Iradier's expedition turned into one of territorial acquisition. Signing hundreds of treaties with chiefs representing tens of thousands of people, the three explorers annexed 13,300 square kilometres in less than two months. First Iradier, then Montes de Oca was taken ill and compelled to return. Ossorio raced on. By the time he had finished, 50,000 square kilometres had been staked out for Spain. In Madrid, Iradier received a hero's welcome. The two-volume record of his travels was a bestseller in its day, but the euphoria was to perish suddenly.

While Iradier's party had roamed around the Equator, others decided the future shape of the African continent. From November 1884 to February 1885, representatives of fourteen nations gathered in Berlin. Instructed to bargain, the Spanish delegation began with a claim of 300,000 square kilometres, pointing out that the El Pardo Treaty had granted them 800,000. The conference agreed to give the Spanish 180,000. Germany agreed not to extend Kamerun south of the Río Campo, but French claims extended north to that river. Thus, the Spanish were given a vast area but excluded from the entire coast.

After years of vehement Spanish protest, a Franco-Spanish Commission was established. It was agreed that King Christian IX of Denmark should arbitrate. But mediation never took place for history struck Spain a damaging blow. On 15 February 1898, the American battleship *Maine* mysteriously exploded while at anchor in Havana harbour. The short, but costly and distracting, war which followed resulted in the loss of all of Spain's remaining colonies in the Western Hemisphere and Asia. Nonetheless, for the first time, those who mattered in Madrid turned their eyes to Africa, and commercial considerations also entered the policy-making process. The last half of the 19th century saw a dramatic rise in the world demand for cocoa. Attractive profits brought Catalonian planters to Fernando Po. But labour was a limiting factor and the Spanish government looked to the continent for a solution.

It was not until 1900 that the Spanish and French were able to sit down to iron out their difficulties. Paris had the upper hand and only 26,000 square kilometres were conceded to Spain, including the northwestern corner of Gabon and the islands of the Muni Estuary. In terms of the size of most European holdings in Africa, this enclave was minuscule. Ruler-straight borders were drawn with Spanish Río Muni hemmed in by the Río Campo to the north, the Río Utamboni to the south, 10° 30′ to the east and the Atlantic to the west. Madrid was really no longer the capital of a colonial power in the same sense as any of the other imperial nations of Europe.

Following the defeat of the Germans in Kamerun in 1916-17, a unique refugee situation occurred. German troops, planters, businessmen and some 60,000 African soldiers and villagers sought refuge in Spanish Guinea. They were the only large group of Europeans ever to become refugees on the African continent. Some of the African leaders wanted to maintain German rule in their country and petitioned the King of Spain to help them, but to no avail. By the end of 1919 the refugees had dispersed, and Kamerun became a League of Nations mandate, partly British but mostly French. However, German influence in the region continued with the presence of German companies and some settlers, and some German associations with the eastern shore of the Gulf of Guinea have survived to this day.

The colonial era to 1947

By this time, large shipping and plantation firms were conducting most of the business in the colony. One Spanish firm with great influence was the Trasatlántica Compañía. Founded in 1850, Trasatlántica had a monopoly on connections with Santa Isabel. The company started the first Spanish messenger steamer service to Santa Isabel in 1888, replacing British and German ships on the same line. In 1898, a new manager, Pedro Bengoa Arriola, arrived at Trasatlántica's Santa Isabel office. He had strong ideas about how Fernando Po should develop. Official Agricultural Chambers (*Cámara Oficial Agrícola*), representing producers, processors and shippers, were set up in the colony to market African produce in Spain. Bengoa became chairman of Fernando Po's *Cámara* and the chamber's general secretary was Juan Bravo Carbonell. Bravo was also a man full of suggestions. He recommended the introduction of banana plantations and suggested moving the colony's capital to Río Benito to give the administration a more central location. His writings are the best and most imaginative pre-Franco works on Spanish Guinea. Bengoa and Bravo moulded the colony's economy. In 1905 Bengoa set up a cattle ranch on Moka, and a few dozen head of cattle grew to over a thousand in a decade. As a great hunter and traveller, Bengoa saw the colony's potential for tourism and safaris, but in 1925, for reasons still unclear, he shot himself. The next year Trasatlántica sold out its Fernando Po holdings to the Compañía Naciónal de Colonización Africana (ALENA) and in 1934, Transmediterránea Company obtained the shipping monopoly. Financed by and connected to the Banco Exterior de España, the most firmly based bank in the colony, ALENA owned various timber and agricultural concessions in Río Muni as well as a coffee plantation and a cattle ranch on Fernando Po.

A few large firms controlled the development of Fernando Po and oversaw the island's plantations. Spanish plantations averaged 56 hectares (compared with African-owned farms which averaged 4.8). As a result of the 1944 Land Act every family was entitled to no less than 4 hectares on which to grow export crops. This was the beginning of the island's dependence on food imports, which has continued to the present.

Río Muni's economy was quite different. Firstly, cacao was unimportant and, unlike neighbouring countries, the enclave did not depend on palm oil. Rubber also proved to be insignificant and only a little over a thousand acres was ever devoted to its cultivation. The enclave's development was based on two commodities: coffee and timber. After the loss of Spain's Latin American territories, and once Río Muni was fully occupied, production rocketed from 9 tonnes in 1917 to 2,451 in 1939 to 6,471 in 1950.

As the mainland is covered almost completely with forests, wood has been a major source of revenue. Europeans were first interested in ebony and mahogany; later, okoumé, available only in Río Muni and Gabon, became the most valued wood. The first large Spanish company began exploiting in 1910 and by 1941 some 103,000 hectares were being lumbered. Several innovations gave added impetus to the Spanish Guinean economy in this century; the rise in demand for coffee and cocoa insured high profits; in 1935 the introduction of the power press brought about a revival in the palm oil trade; and the invention of plywood, for which okoumé is excellently suited, caused a rapid climb in revenues.

Another vehicle of change was Christianity. Portuguese priests had introduced Catholicism to Fernando Po after 1533. Once interest in Africa blossomed in Spain, priests soon followed the traders and explorers. Concerned about Protestant activity on the island, the chaplain of Queen Isabel II, Miguel Martínez y Sanz, was sent to the island and became Santa Isabel's first Apostolic Prefect. A group of Jesuits arrived to combat the spread of Protestantism, but seventeen of their 36 missionaries had died by 1868 when a revolution in Spain forced their return. In 1883, a more lasting missionary effort was begun with the arrival of Claretian missionaries, and two years later the Barcelona-based Conceptionist Sisters started missions on Fernando Po and Corisco.

The section of Spanish Guinean society most open to missionary influence were the Fernandinos. Since their arrival on Fernando Po, they had met with success in almost everything they engaged in. Retail trade, skilled services and plantation management were dominated by them. By the turn of the century the main Fernandino families had become planters. The most prominent Fernandino of all was Maximiliano C. Jones. Jones began his career as a carpentry teacher and subsequently became a plantation foreman and finally a planter himself. He was a Protestant but helped the Claretians to establish themselves. In 1900 he opened a printer's shop in Santa Isabel and slowly acquired more wealth and status than many Europeans on the island. By 1920 Jones was the only African among the colony's ten largest planters. His influence was such that he helped to get the island's first power station built in 1925. After having his seven sons educated in Spain, he retired to his house in the Spanish coastal town of Bilbao.

Bubi society also changed dramatically over the first hundred years of Spanish colonization. During the mid-19th century a king Moka ruled the tribe. Reputed to have lived to be over 100 years old, Moka maintained an isolated life in Riaba and refused to have personal contact with Europeans until 1889. Because of this isolation, many, both at the time and since, believe Moka may have been a series of kings pretending to be one. At this time missionaries sought Bubi converts with little success. On Moka's death, his prime minister, Sas Eburea, seized power and forbade all contact with Europeans. However, the Spanish were too well entrenched to let the Bubi isolate themselves again. Quite a few Bubis on the northern end of Fernando Po had converted to Christianity or formed trade ties with Santa Isabel. Traditional discipline was cracking. After encouraging a tax strike in 1904, Sas Eburea was arrested and taken to Santa Isabel where he fell ill and died. The Spanish claimed he had converted to Catholicism and was baptized on his death-bed.

Moka's successor, Malabo, became king. Tribal order broke down again in June 1910 when Chief Luba of Balacha in southern Fernando Po ordered a rebellion against Spanish labour policies. Spanish troops, advised by none other than Maximiliano C. Jones, put down Luba's clan with great violence. These disturbances were the last acts of resistance by the Bubi; from then on, they worked within the system. Malabo, a weak leader and an alcoholic, died on Moka in 1937. By the time of the last Bubi king's death in 1952, the tribe's traditions had been set aside for the ways of Catholicism and Spanish patronage.

Over the years, the planters persuaded the Bubi to shift from their holdings to less favourable land in exchange for pensions and secondary and higher education scholarships in Spain. Returning students either entered Spanish employment or borrowed money from the combines to establish themselves in a profession. Farms were amalgamated into some fifty plantations totalling 50,000 hectares. The Bubi did some market gardening while the Fernandinos dominated retail commerce. Both island groups were deeply involved in plantation management and in the professions.

Chronically short of manpower, the Spanish cocoa combines needed a workforce for the island. The practice of recruiting Liberian Kru continued, but new malpractices and even outright theft emerged within the corrupt recruitment system. Spain feared the Liberian connection could not be maintained for long and the uncertainty of the situation led in part to the 1926 push into Río Muni's interior. Following the Liberian presidential election of 1927, the defeated candidate, Thomas J. Faulkner, left for the United States where he accused the Liberian government of election irregularities and of condoning the forcible recruitment of labourers for Fernando Po. He claimed work on the island was tantamount to slavery. President C. B. D. King of Liberia denied all accusations and asked the League of Nations to investigate. A commission reported in 1930 that, '. . . a large proportion of the contract labourers shipped to Fernando Po and French Gabon from the southern counties of Liberia have been recruited under conditions of criminal compulsion scarcely distinguishable from slave raiding and slave trading and frequently by misrepresenting the destination.' King resigned, even though he had not been personally criticized and his government had been cleared of most of the other charges.

But Spain was already turning to British-ruled Nigeria, where the crowded Eastern Region had manpower accustomed to migration. A formal Anglo-Spanish labour agreement was signed at the height of the Second World War in 1942. Dissatisfaction among these workers was also high, and despite the crowded and unhealthy barracks housing which was provided, Ibo, Ibibio and Efik contract workers quickly outnumbered all other groups combined.

By the time of Iradier's death in 1911, Río Muni had still not been thoroughly occupied. The Spanish had organized an administration in 1904. However, conditions inland proved quite different and the occupation of the interior really began only with a Spanish expedition in 1926. Ten years later the advance was slowed by the Spanish Civil War. A socialist party, the *Frente Popular* (Popular Front), was formed by about 150 Spaniards in the colony. It was highly influential because within its ranks were both Governor General Luis Sanchez Guerra Saez and Vice-Governor General Porcel. Both the Front and the administration opposed the colony's landowner élite on a number of issues. In September 1936 they were crushed by Spanish troops which Franco had dispatched from the Canaries to Fernando Po. Sanchez was dismissed but Porcel continued the fight on the mainland. The Falangists in control of Fernando Po 'pacified' Republican Río Muni. Franco's forces triumphed after two months, and the *Frente Popular* was no more. Its members had been exiled and its leaders executed. The Spanish naval officer in charge of the repression, Juan Fontan y Lobé, became governor general until 1941. Under his leadership, the push into Río Muni continued. Although expansionists in Franco's government dreamed of an equatorial African empire composed of the Cameroons, Nigeria and Gabon during World War II, the occupation of their own tiny possession was completed only in the late 1940s.

By the end of World War II, Santa Isabel had become a city of importance. Stone buildings and spacious streets bore witness to the island's cocoa wealth. A cathedral was built in 1916. Mediterranean architecture graced the town, giving it the look of Mallorca. Almost half of Fernando Po's residents lived in Santa Isabel, where schools, offices, hospitals, factories and markets ensured a prosperous and secure life for all who co-operated with the Europeans. San Carlos was a banana port, Moka Mountain was a cattle ranching centre and Concepción became something of a holiday resort.

Río Muni was very different. It had a frontier atmosphere, just as active as the island but without the frills. Cultivation had expanded not in the form of plantations but on the basis of smallholdings, the total area of which grew to some 10,000 hectares. Because they were alien to the plantation system and not trusted by the colonial authorities, the Fang were denied employment on Fernando Po. Hence, few Fang were ever able to gain access to Spanish patronage, and those few who did seldom left the mainland.

Virgin Río Muni now began to change. The Ndowe, particularly the Benga, were Christianized early. In 1850, an American Presbyterian missionary, James Love Mackey, founded a mission on Corisco and began the first scientific study of the Benga. He was followed by Robert Hamill Nassau. Arriving in Río Muni with his wife in 1861, Nassau was a doctor, folklore expert, clergyman and, like Mackey, a linguist. He explored Río Muni with great curiosity. Nassau left for Gabon in 1871, having completed a Benga translation of the Bible and several books on the region. In 1868 a Benga named Ikenge Ibia became the first African Christian clergyman in the colony. Trained at an American Presbyterian college, Ikenge took charge of the Corisco mission. A good indication of the degree of Spanish paternalism is the fact that it was not until sixty years after Ikenge's ordination that a Bubi, Joaquin Maria Sialo, became the first Spanish Guinean African to become a Roman Catholic priest. The uncertainty of Río Muni's status led to a dearth of Catholic missionary activity in the early days of Spanish rule. From 1885 to 1904 French and Spanish authorities argued over whether Río Muni should fall under the Vicariate of Gabon or that of Fernando Po. After the Vatican settled the issue in favour of the Spanish, missionary activities in Río Muni were given more attention.

Introduction

Spanish colonialism now impacted upon the Fang and rapid transformations followed: trade changed from barter to cash; manufactured goods demolished the remaining handicraft skills and disrupted the circulation of marriage payments; irreversible disorganization took place. The Fang became victims of trade dependence and with this came inflation, unrest and even greater technological regression. Like many other Bantu peoples, the Fang paid little attention to farming, which was an almost purely female activity – the men traded, hunted and pursued the sport of mock warfare. However, as the cash economy spread, more and more men went to work in timberyards and on plantations, new crops were introduced, and the population became more settled and houses were built for permanence. But not all was well.

In spite of close family ties, migration to do waged labour added a burden to the Fang social system which it could not bear. The tribe underwent an identity crisis. Suspicion and superstition surfaced. Rapid development led to a belief in the white man's ability to perform miracles and subsequently fostered attempts to counter-act the 'Europeans' medicine'. Misunderstandings on the part of both the Spanish and the Fang were the rule rather than the exception. The Spanish built model villages and a good road network and succeeded in improving health conditions. The Fang were awe-struck by these innovations but soon came to suspect them. On the other hand, the Spanish, Ndowe and the island peoples admired the fierceness, independence, energy and intelligence of the Fang and although they failed to notice Fang society's growing problems until very late, they too had their doubts.

Spanish missionaries pushed into the interior. A generation gap emerged among the Fang between the village elders who subscribed to the ancestor-worshipping Bieri cult and the shifting young workers who were influenced by the missionaries. Slowly, Christianity replaced old beliefs, but in some remote areas, the missionary activity backfired and the result was the Bwiti cult, a syncretistic sect which combined Christianity and traditional beliefs in a way quite similar to the Voodoo cults of Haiti. Appearing first in Gabon, it drew displaced labourers and soldiers to its ranks and spread north into Río Muni and Cameroon. But the cult's influence extended far beyond its formal membership.

During the 1940s the Fang attempted, with a good deal of success, to unite their clans under the *alar ayong* movement. This messianic movement, connected with the Bwiti, served as a self-defence organization and as a point of contact and exchange. With a structure like the Mau Mau and lengthy initiation ceremonies believed to involve human sacrifices, the *alar ayong* spread from its original home in Cameroon to Río Muni and Gabon. Protected by its secretive behaviour and by the perpetual lack of understanding on the part of the authorities, it became extremely chauvinistic and politicized. Noting its implications for Gabon, the French quickly suppressed the *alar ayong* in their colonies, as the chauvinism and terrorism which characterized the movement caused tribal disputes and general disorder. Worried by the lack of European-educated leaders in the *alar ayong*, the French began co-opting Fang leaders into the mainstream of Gabonese life. The Gabonese groups emerged into the open, became less anti-French and allowed outsiders to join in, provided they underwent toned-down initiation ceremonies. Members participated in the elections which paved the way to independence, and so in 1960, the French were able to hand Gabon over to a Fang, Léon Mba, and still feel their interests were secure, as they have remained ever since. But the Spanish did nothing to alter their paternalism and the country's real issues were often clouded.

The most important institution of colonial rule in Spanish Guinea was the appropriately named *Patronato de Indígenas* or Native Patronage organization. Headed by the bishop of Santa Isabel, the *Patronato* was originally intended to protect the Bubi. However, after reforms (in 1928 and 1938), this non-governmental organization became almost a government unto itself. It acquired properties and businesses; provided legal assistance for blacks; and ran almost all of the colony's press and educational system. Financed by the Spanish government and by a special tax on cacao and coffee exports, the *Patronato* worked with the administration to formulate colonial policy, often as the senior partner in this relationship. It controlled the lives and futures of Spanish Guineans in ways neither trading firms nor colonial officials were able to.

The schools, hospitals, orphanages and welfare institutions of Spanish Guinea was almost completely in the hands of the Claretians and Conceptionists up to the time of independence. Post-primary education in the colony was neglected and dependence was further ensured by sending the best students to Spain. Until 1943 it was virtually impossible for an African to continue past primary school without leaving the colony. Nevertheless, primary education was free and was extended to all parts of Fernando Po and Río Muni.

Emancipation was a key instrument of Spanish colonial policy. The colonists divided the population into *emancipados* (assimilated citizens) and *menores* (minors, which included all regarded as primitives). Emancipation was granted to natives with higher education, with salaries over 500 pesetas a year or with posts in the civil service. These restrictions meant virtually all Fernandinos, many

Introduction

Bubi and Ndowe and almost no Fang were emancipated before World War II. The *emancipado*, who had to be Christian, benefited in numerous ways: he could be heard in Spanish courts, as opposed to native tribunals, and he was no longer obliged to work on plantations, for emancipation opened many doors for employment and trade. The *Patronato* and the missions, both of which distributed emancipation certificates, controlled this entire system until its dissolution in 1960.

Colonialism in Spanish Guinea rested on three pillars: commercial interests, the Church and the administration. Of these, the last was clearly the weakest and least organized. Noting Spain's turbulent history in the past two centuries, perhaps this should be expected. At the apex of this system was the governor general. He was usually a naval officer and almost always appointed in Madrid by decree. In theory, he was almost omnipotent, but in practice he often had to rely on the *Patronato* or the trading sector for resources, expertise and goodwill. Ninety-nine men held the post of governor general from 1858 to 1968, many with terms cut short because of illness, death or political changes.

There were several administrative bodies to assist the governor general. One of these was the *Dirección de Agricultura* which supervised agriculture. Its head from 1940 to 1961, Jaime Nosti Nava, wrote some 75 books and major articles on the colony and could be described as the outstanding post-World War II expert on Spanish Guinea. There were courts in the colony, but for the most part, decisions were made by administrators at various levels. Few powers of government were separated. The colony had several uniformed security forces; among those deployed were naval infantry, *Guardia Civil* (Spanish Civil Guard) and a local police force known as the *Guardia Colonial*.

In 1945, the *Instituto de Estudios Africanos* (Institute of African Studies) was established in Madrid. Over the years to independence when it was amalgamated with the Spanish Foreign Ministry, this institute conducted and published some excellent research on the colonies, in spite of its marked biases. Many entries in this bibliography are works sponsored by the Institute. However, this knowledge had little effect on the *Dirección General de Marruecos y Colonias* (Spanish Colonial Office), which kept a watchful eye but seemed to understand little. The problems of the colony, particularly among the Fang, had been left to develop to such a degree of complexity that by the 1940s, mere understanding was no comfort at all.

Under Franco, Spanish administration was reorganized. The functions of officials were clarified. Heavy emphasis was placed on efficiency, particularly in the area of economic regulation. Higher land prices and selling by auction put greater acreage in European hands. But Africans were still able to have a stake in the economy by organizing co-operatives, and with total budgets reaching $600,000 by the mid-1960s, local agricultural co-operatives became serious competitors to large landowners.

In Río Muni a large number of Spanish companies established themselves. Coffee was marketed in a more competitive atmosphere than cacao, with 75% of production originating from smallholdings. Looking at the colonial economy of Spanish Guinea, one is led to believe that Fernando Po and especially Río Muni were models of the free-market economy. Not only were many Spanish and African interests in the field, but many older British and German companies were still conducting large volumes of business in the Spanish territories. However, underneath this fa?F2?ûade was a network of monopolies in a few important areas, and a number of restrictive organizations which directed the production of and trade in almost all goods.

The strict Falangist General José Díaz de Villegas y Bustamente was made head of the *Dirección General de Marruecos y Colonias* in 1944 and director of the *Instituto de Estudios Africanos* the following year. Together with Admiral Luis Carrero Blanco, Díaz de Villegas dominated Spanish colonial policy for three decades. Spanish Guinea's economy expanded, but its administration remained authoritarian and primitive. Dissatisfaction with the system increased both within the administration in Santa Isabel and among educated Africans outside government circles.

The twilight of colonialism

Matters came to a head in 1947 during the term of Governor General Juan María Bonelli Rubio. Like most of his predecessors, Bonelli Rubio was a naval officer. He sided with Franco during the Civil War, was appointed Secretary of the Admiralty afterwards and in 1943 he was named governor general. As a shareholder in plantations and banks, Bonelli Rubio seemed to be the ideal appointee. One of Bonelli's subordinates, Heriberto Alvarez García, the Inspector General of Education endeavoured to improve education in the colony. Better teachers were recruited and the training of African teachers was increased from six months to five years. He felt strongly that the salaries of teachers should be raised. In proposing these adjustments, Alvarez García risked accusations of radicalism. Nevertheless, he persisted, and to the surprise of many, Bonelli Rubio backed his proposal. Teachers in the colony demonstrated in support of Alvarez and Bonelli. In a fit of rage, Díaz de Villegas dismissed them both.

Shortly after the salary increase controversy began, a number of *emancipados* organized an anti-colonial movement known as the *Cruzada Nacional de Liberación de Guinea Ecuatorial* (the National Crusade for Equatorial Guinean Liberation – CNLGE). Among the leaders of the CNLGE were a Cameroonian Fang planter – Acacio Mañe, a Fang from Mikomeseng – Enrique Nvó Okenve, and a Fernandino teacher – Marcos Ropo Uri. Madrid attempted to quiet this opposition with small concessions: after 1952 the two Official Agricultural Chambers accepted African members; in 1956 Fernandino patrician Jeremias Barleycorn was appointed mayor of Santa Isabel. However, such morsels of power did little to stem local demands.

In 1950 Mañe presided over an angry meeting of teachers whose petitions for higher salaries had been ignored. Mañe travelled to all corners of Río Muni campaigning for the *Cruzada*. One who heard his words was a young seminarian, Atanasio Ndongo Miyone. After participating in a student strike, Ndongo Miyone fled to Gabon where he joined the police force and married one of León M'ba's daughters. As a member of the CNLGE, he lived the life of a smuggler, campaigning clandestinely in the border towns and travelling throughout west Africa.

Having been admitted to the United Nations in 1955, the Spanish needed to pay at least lip-service to decolonization if they were ever to retrieve Gibraltar from the British. The *Cruzada* would not let the international community ignore Spanish Guinea. Shortly after the arrival in New York of Spain's first UN ambassador, Mañe, Nvó Okenve and Ndongo Miyone sent a memorandum to the UN Secretary General in which they accused Spain of usurping the territory and rights of their people. Because of this memorandum, the eyes of the world were drawn to the colony, much to the anger of Madrid. The UN Decolonization Committee began to debate the status of Spanish colonies.

CNLGE's activities prompted fierce reactions from the colonial administration. Organizations defending African rights in even the remotest sense were proscribed. Public meetings were banned. The authorities maintained a web of spies and thugs. Many were quieted and others went into exile. But in spite of the fear which swept the colony, Acacio Mañe refused either exile or silence. On 20 November 1958, he was arrested in Bata and killed while in detention. In a vain attempt to avoid discovery, his body was thrown into the sea. Hundreds of anti-colonial activists from all tribes departed for neighbouring countries. But the Spanish were not content to leave the anti-colonial groups merely scattered. To intimidate the activists, they sent agents into Cameroon to assassinate Enrique Nvó Okenve on the first anniversary of the death of Mañe. Nvó was murdered a day later.

The CNLGE's leadership eventually passed into the hands of a Bubi lawyer, Luis Maho Sikacha, who soon fled to Cameroon where he joined Ndongo Miyone. The situation in the colony looked hopeless for the opponents of colonialism, but the 'winds of change' blowing across the continent were to make continued Spanish presence untenable. Impetus in this direction came from the granting of independence to all countries around the Spanish possessions in 1960. These new nations, particularly Gabon, applied increasing pressure on Spain. Fang marriage ties proved to be important as many activists had relatives in powerful positions in Gabon and Cameroon. In many ways, the rectangular borders of Río Muni were little more than paper formalities; no amount of patrolling could effectively watch the jungle around the colony's boundaries.

In response to the criticism levelled against Spanish colonialism, the Franco government introduced 'provincialization' in 1960, and Fernando Po and Río Muni were made provinces of Spain. The concept of emancipation was abandoned and the colony's people became Spanish citizens. The *Patronato*'s functions were taken over by the territories' first system of local government. However, both the local government bodies and other new provincial organizations had little power and even less effect. Spanish Guinea was still run by a tiny group of officials. Provincialization was an illusion which allowed the Spanish to continue as before. The one significant development was the allocation to Spanish Guinea of six seats in the Spanish parliament. Hence with the opening of its 1960 session, the *Cortes* saw the seating of colonial representatives for the first time, three of the new members were Africans.

Provincialization added a new dimension to the differences between the largely Westernized island and the less developed mainland. Officially, Spanish Guinea was divided into two provinces. This could be interpreted as being one or two colonies. Indeed, Europeans and Africans alike argued over their status. Many islanders doubted the wisdom of independence while many of the anti-colonial movements had a distinctly Fang character. A colony of two clearly different parts had evolved. Paradoxically, Fernando Po, one of the first places in Africa to see European penetration, was paired with Río Muni, probably the last area on the continent to be fully explored. The Fang outnumbered all other groups combined. In 1960 the population of Spanish Guinea included about 20,000 Bubi,

Introduction

3,000 Fernandinos, 6,000 whites, 35,000 Nigerian workers, 170,000 Fang and about 20,000 others (including Ndowe). However, as throughout most of Africa, national divisions would not be debated and solved locally.

The politics of independence

The granting of provincial status satisfied neither the exiles who had become increasingly nationalistic nor the growing number of African delegates at the United Nations. Appeals for independence were made to the UN every year after 1958 and numerous resolutions were passed asking the Spanish to prepare a timetable for self-government.

The CNLGE was dissolved following quarrels between Ndongo Miyone and Maho Sikacha, and in its place, numerous movements arose. Prominent among these organizations was the *Idea Popular de Guinea Ecuatorial* (IPGE). Its leader, Perea Epota, was made leader of an anti-colonial coalition in Ambam, Cameroon in February 1963. But rifts soon developed within IPGE. The group had developed close ties with Cameroonian nationalist organizations and one wing of the organization supported the idea of a federation with Cameroon. At the IPGE congress of August 1963 proposals for federation were tabled. As a result, opponents of this proposition broke away to form the *Movimiento de Unión Nacional* (MUN). Meanwhile, Ndongo Miyone transformed the rump of the Cruzada into a leftist group called the *Movimiento Nacional de Liberación de Guinea Ecuatorial* (MONALIGE).

A new movement based in Gabon, the *Movimiento de Unión Popular de Liberación de la Guinea Ecuatorial* (MUPGE) joined forces with MUN to create the *Movimiento de Unión Nacional de Guinea Ecuatorial* (MUNGE). This party was encouraged by the Spanish authorities and planters as an alternative to the strident nationalism of IPGE and MONALIGE. The leadership of MUNGE quickly passed to MUPGE's president, Bonifacio Ondo Edu, a Fang planter. Ondo Edu had fled Río Muni after the murder of Mañe, but he had returned during provincialization to become mayor of his home town. As leader of MUNGE, he freed the organization of Cameroonian influence.

Around this time Spanish policy changed. Prisoners were freed and many exiles returned. In response to criticism from many quarters, the Spanish government announced it would let the people of Spanish Guinea decide whether or not the colony should be self-governing. An autonomy plan was prepared and on 15 December 1963 the choice of continued status as two provinces or unity under an autonomous government was put to a referendum. The division between the island and the mainland became blatantly obvious. In fear of Fang domination, the citizens of Fernando Po voted 7,163 to 4,440 against autonomy while Río Muni polled 58,163 to 22,823 in favour. As the vote was counted on a colony-wide basis, autonomy was approved by a 66% poll.

The autonomy plan called for self-rule in domestic affairs only. An *Asamblea General* (General Assembly) was formed. This body of nineteen members (eight from Fernando Po and eleven from Río Muni) was to be the legislature of the colony and its presidency was to alternate annually between the two provinces. However, the *Asamblea* had limited powers and its real influence lay in its role as the elector of the *Consejo de Gobierno* (Governing Council). The *Consejo* was a cabinet of eight members (four from each province). It prepared all bills and budgets and supervised enforcement. Its president was nominated by a one-third vote of the *Consejo* and then appointed by decree from Madrid. The first, and only, *Consejo* president was Ondo Edu, who was immediately denounced by the exiles. A number of other changes came with the granting of autonomy: the governor general became a commissioner general with substantially less power but still holding a veto over the *Asamblea*; the colony also no longer contributed to the Spanish budget. During the first few months of 1964, elections were held for almost all offices, and this time all six members sent to the *Cortes* were Africans.

During the autonomy period, the conflict of interests between the islanders and the Fang took on new dimensions as it became apparent that the Spanish were going to bow to international demands for independence, and that the union of the two provinces into one entity was more than probable. All the motives for Spain insisting on keeping Fernando Po and Río Muni tied together are still not clear. Undoubtedly, many felt the creation of one small state was better than the establishment of two even smaller ones. Others viewed Río Muni almost as if it was a dependency of Fernando Po. Historically, this may have been valid, but there was little if any economic integration between the two. Fernando Po acquired its imports from Spain, its labour force from Nigeria and its markets from various European nations, usually via Spain. Río Muni, on the other hand, looked to Gabon and Cameroon. Admittedly, many of its imports came from Spain, but these were supplied not through Santa Isabel, but through the mainland port of Bata. The cacao cultivation system of Fernando Po had different needs from the economy which had developed in Río Muni, where timber, coffee and palm oil had become important. The only reason the two territories were together at all was the fact that they had the same colonial master.

Introduction

The rise of Francisco Macías Nguema

A new leader came to the forefront: Francisco Macías Nguema. Although he claimed Nsangayong in Mongomo District as his home, he was probably born in Oyen in Gabon. His father, Biyogo was a well-known witch-doctor, notorious for the murder of one of his sons. Macías was a shy boy, dominated by his elder brother, and was a very poor student. He failed civil service examinations three years in a row before being hired as a servant by the administration. Passing the examination on his fourth try in 1944, he took a posting as an orderly in the forestry service. Later he moved on to the position of clerk in the Department of Public Works in Bata. In 1950 he became an *emancipado* and two years later, he was posted to the district of Mongomo as an assistant court interpreter.

Inability to understand what was happening socially and politically in Río Muni is frequently cited as the single most important shortcoming of the Spanish authorities. Perhaps nowhere is this more clearly demonstrated than in Macías' career in Mongomo. Although his position in the colonial establishment was low, Macías used his skills without scruples. He freely twisted his translations for or against people for his own profit. Noting the 'respect' people seemed to show him, the Spanish made him mayor of Mongomo. Macías was made Deputy President and Head of Public Works in the *Consejo* in 1964. While anti-colonial militants were in exile, Macías carried on as a puppet of Spain. During his term on the *Consejo*, he became fully aware of his lack of education and an inferiority complex began to root itself deeply. He resented those in authority over him, namely the Spanish and Ondo Edu. He also grew to dislike Santa Isabel. His amazingly rapid promotion from assistant interpreter to mayor to deputy president, all in one year, only added to his problems.

Meanwhile, the Spanish government announced that a constitutional conference would be convened in October 1967 to lay down the basic code of laws for a new nation to be called Equatorial Guinea. The African delegation was composed of forty-one members representing the colony's interest groups. The IPGE, MONALIGE, MUNGE and Unión Bubi (a Bubi separatist party), all sent delegates. The Spanish delegation was led by Díaz de Villegas.

As a *Consejo* minister, Macías was present at the conference and clearly illustrated what Equatorial Guinea could expect from him. His talk was incoherent fury with constant appeals to the chairman to allow him to finish. He expressed no political ideology and had no programme. One commentator referring to Macías' speeches wrote, 'They defy analysis of his political thought and leave the reader as confused as Macías sometimes declared himself to be.' In a speech which he made at the conference in 1967, Macías proclaimed Hitler to be the liberator of Africa while arguing for independence on left-wing nationalist terms, thus displaying his fascination with both extremes of the political spectrum.

It is not surprising that Macías visited several doctors and psychiatrists. He had considerable trouble with his hearing and went to Madrid's Clinica Ruber for examination and treatment. The diagnosis obviously revealed more than physiological symptoms for he was then sent to a Barcelona psychiatrist. His deafness increased and three years later he secretly returned to Barcelona for further consultations. This is one explanation for the screaming and shouting which were to become hallmarks of his speeches.

Macías did not make a great impact on the other participants at the conference. However, he did impress a Spanish law professor named José Antonio García Trevijano Fos. He saw great potential in Macías and, as his adviser, García groomed the witch-doctor's son for great things from which he too could profit.

The conference was suspended when dissent between unionists and separatists caused a deadlock. The Unión Bubi remained adamantly against association with Río Muni. Debates were bitter and a pause was essential. During the suspension, Macías visited the United Nations in New York. This trip was purely for domestic consumption, for, as he later admitted, he suffered language problems and was able to communicate with very few people. In one of the trivial incidents which gain prominence in an impressionable mind, Macías met two Puerto Rican janitors in a hallway at the UN. They told him they were being oppressed, and this was the root of an anti-American bias which was to intensify.

Macías returned to his country with an enhanced reputation. At this stage Spain needed little prompting to act on Equatorial Guinean independence. The Spanish resumed the conference in April 1968 and set dates for both general elections and independence. Macías and García had used the adjournment wisely. A group named the *Secretariado Conjunto* had been formed around Macías, composed of IPGE members and marginal elements of MUNGE and MONALIGE and financed by García Trevijano.

The Spanish government pushed the conference ahead. A constitution was hastily drafted and included the features which have become common to most constitutions. Universal adult suffrage was reaffirmed and the autonomy of each province was also guaranteed. Each province was to be given a provincial council: Fernando Po's council was composed of eight members with one for Annobón; Río Muni's twelve-member council had a seat reserved for Corisco and another for the Elobeyes. At the nationwide level there was a bicameral legislature. The lower house, the *Asamblea de la República*, had 36 deputies elected for five-year terms. The seats were apportioned as a result of a political compromise, with 15 going to Fernando Po, 19 to Río Muni and 2 to Annobón. The members of the *Asamblea* were divided into twelve committees, roughly corresponding to ministerial portfolios. The upper house or *Consejo de la Republica* was composed of six members elected for four-year terms and was mainly concerned with examining the constitutionality of laws, arbitrating conflicts of jurisdiction, and nominating judges. The leadership of the new *Consejo* alternated annually between Fernando Po and Río Muni.

Executive power was vested in a president and a cabinet. Mirroring the Falangist régime in Madrid, the Equatorial Guinean head of state was given broad constitutional powers. He appointed the Vice President and half of the cabinet (the other half was appointed by the provincial councils). The President had the rights to dissolve the *Asamblea*, to suspend basic civil rights for two weeks, to confirm motions of censure against ministers, and to cancel any decision of either provincial council after informing the Supreme Court. Because of the divided nature of the cabinet's appointment, its effectiveness was subject to strong political unity on the national level. But this cohesion did not exist and in its absence an already strong president could increase his power. The proposed constitution provided for budgets every two years and as budgets required two-thirds vote of the *Asamblea*, agreement between Fernando Po and Río Muni was necessary.

As Bubi separatism seems to have been a stumbling-block at the conference, most of the compromises benefited Fernando Po. Although the island accounted for only a little over 10% of the new nation's total population, 42% of the assembly seats, the vice-presidency and what amounted to a veto over budgets were conceded to the island. In one of his few clear statements at the conference, Macías went on record opposing these compromises and advocating the division of the two provinces of Equatorial Guinea into separate nations, if the confusing system provided by the proposed constitution was the only other alternative. He was voted down. Paradoxically, the constitution gave political and administrative concessions to the islanders but offered little legal protection for minorities. Although the constitution was accepted by the *Cortes*, eighty members of that body signed a declaration expressing concern about minority rights.

On 11 August 1968, the constitution was presented to the people of Equatorial Guinea in a UN-monitored referendum. 64.3% approved, but the vote on Fernando Po was confused. Officially, the islanders accepted union under the new constitution by 4,763 votes to 4,486. However, reports from other monitors provide good reason to believe the 'noes' exceeded the 'yeas' by 218.

The leadership of the new nation was now the only question. García Trevijano put up 50 million pesetas to finance Macías. He wrote his speeches and masterminded his presidential election campaign. Macías was to run against Ondo Edu (MUNGE), Atanasio Ndongo Miyone (MONALIGE) and Edmundo Bosio Dioco (Unión Bubi); all of whom were more popular, more experienced and better educated than him. However, with García's help Macías ran a brilliant campaign. While his opponents debated the degree of future collaboration with Spain, Macías presented himself as the only true nationalist. The ideas put forward in his campaign speeches did not match his past as a faithful colonial servant. Posters and leaflets, printed in Spain by García Trevijano, promised everything to everybody. Macías carefully covered his lack of education by appealing to tradition. He concentrated on rural Río Muni, travelling widely and meeting local chiefs. His message was simple: follow me and I will rid the country of foreigners and their 'magic' will be ours.

As in many Third World countries where illiteracy is high, the candidates in Equatorial Guinea chose symbols to identify themselves. One of the most successful tactics of Macías' campaign was the use of a tiger symbol. The fact that the tiger does not exist in Africa made it even more mystically powerful and attractive to the villagers of Río Muni. Symbolism is greatly significant to the Fang whose language has an amazingly large vocabulary of abstract philosophical concepts. Macías knew this enigmatic side well and was more than willing to add a new creature to Fang mythology.

In Santa Isabel, Macías went on television, a seemingly miraculous medium to the average Equatorial Guinean. He emanated an entirely different image from the one he presented on the mainland. Here was a serious politician, a man who had gone to Madrid and New York to ensure his people's freedom. His reputation shot up. But the fame of Bonifacio Ondo Edu was also considerable and Macías might have lost had it not been for the blundering support given to his opponents by the Spanish authorities. This interference would not be forgotten.

On election day, 22 September 1968, Macías emerged with 36,716 votes, Ondo Edu with 31,941 and the remaining 24,299 votes were divided among the other two candidates. No one won a clear majority and so a second round of balloting was scheduled for the following week. Ndongo Miyone offered to exclude Macías from power by allying his party with MUNGE. But Ondo Edu, assuming he could win by himself, refused to make any deal with MONALIGE. Ndongo threw his support to Macías. Hoping to gain some major cabinet posts, Bosio Dioco's Unión Bubi also ordered its members to vote for Macías. Participation in the second ballot on 29 September was higher and Macías won a resounding victory over Ondo. As the election was carefully monitored by the UN, there is little doubt the people of Equatorial Guinea had made their choice. However, the composition of Macías' electoral opposition is well worth noting. As both events and refugee surveys were later to show, a large majority of intellectuals, teachers, doctors, lawyers, engineers and clergymen were strongly opposed to Macías. As this opposition made itself felt in the early days of his régime, the new president's inferiority complex was aggravated.

The days during and immediately after the polling were marked by intrigue. The membership of Macías' cabinet was clearly dictated to him by the Spanish and due to the complex 'safeguards' built into the system both Macías' allies and opponents had a word in cabinet appointments. The result was a cabinet which represented a very broad range of interests. Bosio Dioco was made Vice-President and Minister of Commerce. Ndongo Miyone became Foreign Minister. A MONALIGE dissident and cousin of Macías, Angel Masie Ntutumu, was given the post of Minister of the Interior. The lone Fernandino in the cabinet was Minister of Agriculture Agustin Grange Molay. The Unión Bubi also received the labour portfolio which went to Roman Boricho Toichoa. The IPGE was given only one post, the Ministry of Health headed by Pedro Ekong Andeme. Without even knowing the basics of law, a Colonial Guard officer Jesus Eworo Ndongo was made Minister of Justice. In addition to posts in the cabinet other positions were given on a broad basis. Bubi leader Enrique Gori Molubuela became a Fernando Po provincial councillor and first secretary at the Foreign Ministry. Bubi chief Torao Sikara was made President of the *Asamblea*. Two days after the composition of the cabinet was announced, on 12 October 1968, Equatorial Guinea was declared an independent nation and became a member of the United Nations shortly afterwards. However, Equatorial Guinea never became party to the Geneva Conventions or set up a national Red Cross society until the 1980s.

Conditions at independence

It would be grossly unfair to assert that all Spanish activity was designed to promote neo-colonialism after independence. Many Spaniards liked their African subjects and showed very little racism towards those who had become *emancipados*. The last decade of

Spanish rule saw a serious attempt to heal the economic wounds of the past, and much money was put into developing the economic and social infrastructure of the colony.

In 1965 Fernando Po's per capita GNP was US$466, by far the highest in black Africa. Río Muni was not nearly as prosperous. Nevertheless, the per capita GNP for the entire country climbed to US$300 by independence. The literacy rate was 89% and energy consumption was the fourth highest in black Africa. In 1960 the colony's per capita export index was the highest in Africa at US$135 (Ghana's was $48 and South Africa's $87). Fernando Po had 12.3 telephones per 1,000 inhabitants. Government radio stations had been built in Santa Isabel and Bata and private broadcasting companies transmitted local programmes in Santa Isabel and around the Muni Estuary. Roads in both parts of the country were good and increasing numbers of vehicles were evident. In 1963 an international airport was finished near Santa Isabel. The Spanish completed a television station, and by the time of the conclusion of the Constitutional Conference, the Spanish had built one of the highest transmitters in Africa on the Pico de Santa Isabel. One the the last Spanish gifts given to the colony were free television sets installed in public places, instruments which served Macías well during his campaign.

Thanks to the missions, education was much better in 1968 than it had been ten years earlier. But in higher education, the emphasis was still on going to Spain. More than 80 Equatorial Guineans were sent to Spain for schooling each year. A quarter of these were for postgraduate studies. Health conditions were also greatly improved by the Spanish. In Río Muni the battle against the tsetse fly was being won – in the 1920s there were thousands of victims of sleeping sickness while by 1942 their number was reduced to 538, and fourteen years later several hundred thousand analyses revealed only 70 cases. Tropical syphilis and malaria were also successfully controlled. At Mikomeseng in northern Río Muni, the largest leper sanitoriums cared for an average of 1,210 patients after treating as many as 3,000 in 1955. Having had four to five thousand lepers in the 1940s, freedom from the disease was within reach, and leprosy-related deaths had declined to eight in 1962. There was one doctor per 7,230 inhabitants. In 1967 the country had sixteen hospitals with 1,637 beds, which made the Equatorial Guinean ratio of hospital beds per capita better than Spain's.

The capital and main cacao port, Santa Isabel, had virtually all the luxuries of a European city. Its Spanish architecture and increasing wealth made it unique on the west coast of Africa. But the capital was not the only developed area in the country. San Carlos had become a thriving banana port. The whole island from its shores to its peaks enjoyed a high standard of living. Río Muni had also progressed. Its chief city, port and capital, Bata had lost its rough edges. Growing from a settlement of 237 inhabitants in 1901, Bata had become the mainland enclave's major port, displacing the Muni Estuary in the process. In 1960 the city had 3,548 inhabitants (1,426 whites) and a number of schools, workshops, barracks, a hospital, a prison, a power station, a wood-veneering factory and numerous offices. The inland towns and villages also felt changes. Missions, hospitals, plantations and lumber camps dotted the province. However, such developments, backed by a bumper cacao crop in 1967, only increased the illusion that all was well. Spanish paternalism had caused untold confusion in the minds of those Africans whose value systems were being transformed. Such attitudes gave rise to inferiority complexes, fixations on Spanish things and undirected resentments toward foreigners. The country was left with severe economic and social cleavages. Its political system was needlessly complicated for a nation of its size. Its leader was a strong-willed man with little education and great psychological handicaps.

Post-independence politics

The arrival of Equatorial Guinean independence was overshadowed by the war in nearby Biafra. Fernando Po with its large numbers of Ibo migrant workers was particularly aware of this conflict as a number of Biafran refugees had sought safety on the island. The International Red Cross had begun relief flights into the rebelling state from Santa Isabel in July 1968. Macías saw this as a threat and, after some pressure from the Nigerian consul, he began a war of nerves with both the Biafrans and the Red Cross. Eventually, relief flights were suspended and the break-away republic was starved into submission.

The internal problems of newly independent Equatorial Guinea were compounded by Spanish interference. The new nation's economy was under the thumb of the settlers and islanders. Not surprisingly, Macías felt Spanish influence deserved immediate attention. From the beginning Macías emphasized his dislike of Fernando Po by conducting most of the government business in Bata. He planned to eject the Spaniards as soon as possible.

After losing the elections, Ondu Edu fled to Gabon believing his life to be in danger. Eager not to offend a new neighbour and with Macías' assurances that his opponent had nothing to fear, the Gabonese extradited Ondo who was quickly placed under house arrest in Equatorial Guinea. He was accused of plotting to overthrow

Macías with the help of some Ibos on Fernando Po. As a result Ondo Edu and three of his closest political associates were imprisoned without charge or trial. Within days the MUNGE leader and his three 'accomplices' were killed. But these deaths were only the tip of an iceberg. Around the country, numerous opponents of the régime were killed or imprisoned.

Macías turned to the problem of the Spanish. In a series of violent speeches at the beginning of 1969, the President encouraged anti-Spanish feelings. He demanded that the number of flags flying over Spanish diplomatic missions in the country should be reduced. The Spanish ambassador refused. On 23 February some National Guardsmen pulled down and burned some flags of the Spanish Consulate-General in Bata and a Spaniard was killed in the fray. The Ministry of the Interior declared that the safety of Spanish citizens could no longer be guaranteed, and Spanish forces in the country were mobilized and occupied the towns and airport of Fernando Po. Macías declared both the ambassador and the consul *personae non gratae* and they were subsequently recalled to Madrid. Spaniards were harassed by gangs. Spanish radio announced on 1 March that paratroops had occupied Santa Isabel and Bata airports. The Equatorial Guinean government declared a state of emergency. The next day about 500 Europeans left Santa Isabel by sea and the British and American staff of Mobil Oil Company's exploration teams were evacuated from Río Muni by air. The Spanish government announced a plan to remove all troops from Equatorial Guinea as soon as Spanish citizens who wished to leave were permitted to do so.

By the evening of 5 March, it became apparent that the *Emergencia*, as the situation became known, had taken a very nasty turn. A number of senior political leaders and cabinet ministers had been arrested following an unsuccessful coup against Macías. Ndongo Miyone was reported to have rallied some National Guardsmen around him who then blew up Bata's radio station and occupied government buildings. Pro-Macías troops counter-attacked and the rebels fled, leaving the Foreign Minister cornered in the cabinet room. There are many contradictory stories as to how he met his death but what is known is that he jumped or was thrown out of the cabinet room window, probably after having both of his legs broken with rifle butts, and then he died of neglect in Bata Prison. Macías announced on 8 March that Ndongo was 'fighting for his life in hospital and would be tried by a "people's court".' Two days later, by which time it is almost certain Ndongo had died, Macías claimed that the Foreign Minister had left Bata Hospital under armed guard. Ndongo Miyone disappeared without any verifiable records.

A reign of terror had begun. Dozens of the country's leaders, both from the government and opposition, were detained and killed. Torao Sikara died of thirst in Bata Jail. Gori Molubuela died of gangrene after his eyes had been gouged out. The Fernandino mayor of Santa Isabel, Balboa Dougan, died in prison under 'unknown circumstances'. The country's incompetent Minister of Justice, Eworo Ndongo, was placed under house arrest and later killed. Former Minister of Agriculture Nsue Nchama was murdered along with his successor. Saturnino Ibongo Iyanga, a youthful schoolteacher and journalist who was Equatorial Guinea's first representative at the United Nations, was recalled 'for consultations'. On arrival at Santa Isabel Airport he was accused of being part of Ndongo's conspiracy, a charge which he refuted. There are also several accounts of his torturous death in jail, but Macías said he committed suicide, and meanwhile the ambassador's replacement in New York went as far as to say his predecessor wasn't even dead. Although Macías stated that only about ten people had been arrested, at least eighteen prisoners died in Bata Hospital alone. Old scores were settled while Equatorial Guineans watched their fledgling democracy die after a life of only 145 days.

Having effectively eliminated most of his potential political rivals, Macías took over the post of Foreign Minister himself. To prevent 'incidents', all weapons were collected. Finally, on 12 March, Macías lifted the state of emergency; its purpose was accomplished. He accused the Franco régime of backing Ndongo. Madrid denied these allegations and cast doubt on Macías' assurances by continuing to press for the return of its citizens. UN representatives met with the Spanish and requested a slow-down of the departure of Europeans from the former colony as the new nation would be deprived of technicians and managers. The cacao crop on Fernando Po would also be in danger and the Nigerian workers had not been paid. But Franco refused, and so on 25 March an exodus began. Río Muni was left with only about eighty European settlers. Once thriving Fernando Po saw all but 8% of its whites flee. Over the decade to come, the number of European residents of all nationalities in both parts of Equatorial Guinea would dwindle to around sixty. Plantations were abandoned by owners. Businesses closed, never to open again. Workers went unpaid. Communications were paralysed. A country once hailed as a potential 'African Switzerland' became a model of stagnation within days.

However, by May 1969, most, if not all, was forgiven. An economic and commercial co-operation agreement was signed between Spain and Equatorial Guinea. Spain agreed to purchase at least 20,000 tonnes of cocoa, 1,850 tonnes of other cacao products, 6,000 tonnes of coffee, 215,500 tonnes of wood and smaller quantities of other agricultural products annually. The Spanish agreed to pay higher prices than normal on the world market, provided Equatorial Guinea sold to no one else until these quotas were filled. For its part the Equatorial Guinean government agreed to give preference to Spanish imports. Duties were set at 30% for Spanish goods and 75% for all others. As a result of this agreement, the country's dependence on Spain was sharply increased. From 1963 to 1967 an average of 65% of all Equatorial Guinean imports came from Spain. In 1970, 80% of all imports were Spanish and 86% of all Equatorial Guinean cocoa and 100% of all exported coffee and wood went to Spain.

Madrid provided assistance to balance the budget. The Franco régime advanced the necessary funds to ensure her ex-colony's admission to the IMF. Personnel were supplied to the new national airline, LAGE, and to run Equatorial Guinea's telecommunications network. A educational aid programme amounting to 7,000,000 pesetas a year was set up. In short, the Spanish gave Macías many of the things which he could use to show his people that Equatorial Guinea was a progressive nation and that he, Macías, was responsible for these developments. The Spanish hoped to retain control, but the day would come when Macías would prove them wrong by dropping out of the world economic system.

The Macías era

As a result of the crises of March 1969, Macías declared that the 1968 Constitution had serious defects. He was able to completely sweep it away with a series of decrees. In May 1971, Legislative Decree No. 415 repealed a number of articles in the Constitution and promulgated a decree allowing the President to dissolve the *Asamblea* at his pleasure. Provisions relating to elections and the removal of the President from office were repealed and a council with purely advisory functions was established. In October 1971, Law No. 1 provided death as the penalty for 'rebellion' and 'offences against territorial integrity' and for any person who threatens, kills or attempts to kill the President or who deprives him of his personal freedom or uses violence or serious intimidation to force him to perform an act against his will. Thousands were to die under suspicion of such charges. Imprisonment of up to twelve years was imposed on those who dared to insult, slander or threaten the President or members of the government. He abolished all political parties and created the *Juventud en Marcha con Macías* (Youth on the March with Macías or JMM), a paramilitary organization. The JMM incorporated into its ranks the thugs who had been used to intimidate the Spanish settlers. This organization was given power to harass anyone outside the highest levels of government and Macías' own clan. Macías also established the *Partido Unico Nacional de Trabajadores* (The Unique National Workers' Party or PUNT). Its symbol was a tiger ready to pounce on its prey. All adults were required to be members and everyone, including children, was compelled to parade weekly with wooden rifles (sold by PUNT at 50 pesetas each).

Executions abounded. Often the entire population of an area would be herded together to hear a trial. 'Defence' lawyers would plead for mercy rather than offer a defence and the inevitable death sentence would be carried out in the form of a public spectacle. In 1969 the crowds were treated to a bungled mass hanging of enemies of the state accompanied by a recording of Mary Hopkin singing 'Those were the Days'. On Christmas Eve of that year, prisoners were publicly shot in Santa Isabel; on later occasions victims were beheaded and their heads were left to rot on poles; live burials and tortures involving fires were also employed. However, beating seems to have been the most common form of execution, particularly in the two major prisons: Bata Jail and Blackbich Prison in Santa Isabel. Assassination became a way of life, as the JMM freely roamed the country. The Bubis, Fernandinos and Ndowe suffered especially. The leadership of the Unión Bubi was decimated. But surprisingly, Bosio Dioco remained Vice-President. At that time he was too powerful and too well known in Spanish circles to be eliminated. Much Fernandino property was destroyed or used to depletion. A great number, if not a majority, of educated people were rounded up and many met grisly fates in prison. As would be discovered in the years to come, the initial sweep of murders and jailings included not only opponents and intellectuals but also their families and sometimes their entire villages. The whole nation was held hostage. Equatorial Guinean students abroad were ordered to return home or lose their citizenship and families. As time went by, Macías' paranoia embraced all tribes and groups.

Macías gradually assumed all legislative, executive, judicial and military powers. His ability to do this lay not only in his own cunning, but also in the lack of any mass political consciousness within Equatorial Guinean society. He formed a political police known as the *Milicia Popular*. Originally multi-tribal, it was eventually dominated by the Mongomo Fang and was a feared instrument of enforcement for PUNT. Pitted against each other as well as against 'enemies' of the state, the three armed forces (the *Guardia Nacional*, the JMM and the Milicia) maintained a constant vigil over the country. Life was very strictly regulated. For example, local security officers issued permits for work, travel and medical treatment and were responsible for the surveillance of all movement within their districts. They monitored travellers as well as their district's residents, and outside the villages, the Militia and the National Guard maintained checkpoints every 25 kilometres, day and night. At each checkpoint there were separate camps for the two services to check on each other as well as on travellers. To make matters still more complicated, the membership of the JMM often interlocked with those of the two security forces.

Contrary to his campaign promises, respect for Fang elders did not return, and old chiefs were replaced by young militants. These new men saw that reporting opposition and discontent had its rewards. Hence all power emanated from the President and Macías was assured of a base of support in which no one dared to look suspicious. PUNT membership became compulsory from birth. Failure to produce the all-important PUNT membership card on demand usually led to arrest. Everyone soon found themselves casting eyes over shoulders before moving or speaking.

Macías' mental condition became extremely unstable. Bubi psychologist Loiri Comba described him as a manic depressive. Macías secretly visited Barcelona, but to no avail. By now his eyesight was failing and he was renowned for smoking marijuana and drinking the little-known hallucinogen, *iboga*. Made from a local tree, *iboga* can be smoked or drunk. Its effects are similar to those of LSD and it plays an important part in Bwiti ceremonies and traditional medicine. These drugs were undoubtedly responsible for some of Macías' incoherence. He began to have nightmares, which often featured in his speeches.

Following the crisis with Spain, Equatorial Guinea virtually dropped out of the news. Macías closed down most of the press, instated severe censorship and banned all foreign journalists. Visas became very difficult to obtain. After 1970 there was not one reliable economic figure, government statistic or census report to be found in the country. Decrees, budget information and administrative memoranda could hardly be called official in any accepted sense of the word. The Franco régime further aided Macías by maintaining strict silence from the very beginning. In January 1971 all news concerning Equatorial Guinea was classified *materia reservada* (reserved material) by the Spanish government. That is to say it was in violation of Spain's Official Secrets Act. Of the nine Africans who had sat in the *Cortes* from 1960 to 1968, six were murdered. By the end of 1974 more than two-thirds of the members of the 1968 Parliament had been executed or were missing. Vice-President Edmundo Bosio Dioco 'committed suicide' after having been arrested following the discovery in his home of an official portrait of Macías torn across a corner. Jesus Buendy, governor of the central bank, was tortured and his village was burned down. Within a year, exiles reported Buendy's death. In March 1973 a cholera epidemic decimated the population of Annobón when the régime refused to provide medical assistance. Macías even tried to sell some islands and a border zone to the Gabonese. Madrid didn't seem to care. Equatorial Guinea was closed and those few parts of the world which even knew of the tiny nation's existence closed their eyes.

The Nigerian workforce proved to be another victim of the terror. In 1972, disliking restrictions imposed by the régime, they began leaving Fernando Po. Ill-treatment of Nigerian embassy officials and workers led to a break in diplomatic relations. Finally the Nigerian government evacuated its citizens. Macías refused to allow locally born wives to accompany their husbands, and the Militia opened fire on the returnees. As a result of the Nigerian evacuation, labour shortages caused massive economic difficulties. Macías instated drastic measures: between 20,000 and 25,000 Río Munians were arrested and sent to the island as forced labour, and later, boys between ages seven and fourteen were drafted for unpaid labour on the plantations and resisting fathers were executed. Since the first forced labour drafts of 1972-73, thousands of Equatorial Guineans had left for Gabon, Cameroon, Nigeria and Spain. Eventually a sixth of the population was forcibly recruited as slave labourers on cacao and coffee plantations and in timber-yards. By 1979, approximately a third of the population fled the country, tens of thousands died, and economic and cultural activity simply ceased. Forced labour, trade loss, political terrorism, and a fishing ban designed to deter potential escapees bankrupted Fernando Po. The island people were denied any significant political rights. To prevent escapes, all were prohibited from going near the shores. Out-going mail was nonexistent for several years. For thousands of Bubis and Fernandinos, there was little chance of becoming refugees.

The refugees in neighbouring countries and throughout Europe formed a number of organizations to publicize their country's plight and seek the ousting of Macías. Most prominent among these has been the Geneva-based *Alianza Nacional de Restoratión Democrática* (ANRD), which has opposed the régime and its successor on many levels, including that of the UN Commission on Human Rights. However, disagreement within the ranks of the opposition and lack of support from abroad rendered most of these movements ineffective.

Macías blamed much of what went wrong in his country on Spanish imperialism and the Catholic Church. He accused the Vatican of intrigue and intimidation in the 1968 elections and of coup attempts

1

since the country's independence. The Vicar of the Bata Diocese, Alberto Maria Ndongo, was killed in prison, and many other clergymen were imprisoned. All foreign priests were deported and the country's two bishops went into exile. All private schools, primarily Catholic ones, were closed. Sermons were censored and heavy fines were imposed on fathers who gave their children Christian names. Next Macías demanded that religious services begin with 'in the name of the President Macías and his son.' Eventually, Macías banned all mass public meetings, including church services. Finally, as of early 1978, all Catholic Church activities were banned and virtually all native-born priests had been imprisoned for participation in such 'illegal' activities as baptisms and funerals. Freedom of religion was completely crushed.

Under Macías, education in Equatorial Guinea became little more than a sham of indoctrination. Parents had no channels through which they could change or even complain of the system. As increasing numbers of children were press-ganged on to plantations, education ceased to exist except for a select few. Macías proclaimed African 'authenticity' to be the national goal and Spanish names were converted to African ones (including his own which reverted to Masie). Santa Isabel became Malabo, San Carlos became Luba, Fernando Po became Masie Nguema Island, Río Muni became Mbini, and so on. On a different level, shortages of certain commodities were explained away by declaring various products to be 'un-African'.

The 3 August 1979 coup

Political executions increased rapidly during 1978 and 1979. Macías' paranoia ruled the nation and alienated some of his staunchest supporters. A breaking-point was reached in June 1979 when eleven National Guard officers were executed in Nsangayong. A nephew of Macías and brother of one of the executed, Lt. Col. Teodoro Nguema Obiang, was commander of the Fernando Po military region and vice-minister of defence. On 3 August 1979, he led a successful *coup d'état* which ousted and arrested Macías after a two-week bloodbath. Macías was tried in a cinema in Malabo and executed on 29 September 1979. He was so feared by his people that his execution had to be carried out by élite Moroccan troops after Equatorial Guinean soldiers refused to involve themselves. He swore his ghost would return to haunt those who had condemned him to death. Macías' name was erased from the many things he had named after himself. Fernando Po was renamed Bioko. Remembering Obiang as a particularly brutal follower of Macías and noting that the new president had eliminated much damning evidence from Macías' trial which would implicate himself and other junta members, ANRD claimed the coup was little more than a 'palace revolution'. The new régime was approached with suspicion by all.

International reactions, 1969-1980

The most shocking feature of the terror which afflicted Equatorial Guinea in the eleven years of Macías' rule was the lack of concern by which the case was obscured. During the Macías era, no national government or international organization took any significant action to stop the oppression beyond issuing a few carefully worded condemnations. Río Muni's neighbours, Cameroon and Gabon, were both afraid of importing Fang nationalism due to the large Fang minorities in their countries. Spain, Equatorial Guinea's major trading partner and aid supplier, did not wish to change the situation to her own disfavour. Relations with the régime grew steadily worse as atrocities increased, but Spain did little to improve the situation. When the news of the August 1979 coup was released, the Spanish government admitted foreknowledge but denied complicity. The French had a ten-year forestry concession in the country and millions of dollars worth of construction contracts. In 1976, the United States broke diplomatic relations with the Macías régime under mysterious circumstances, but the US government provided aid to the country and conducted uranium exploration surveys in Equatorial Guinea after the break, fearing increased Soviet influence. Macías cultivated close ties with the Soviet bloc to humiliate the Spanish. The Soviet Union, which had a most-favoured-nation trade pact with Equatorial Guinea, had unlimited fishing rights in Equatorial Guinean waters. A large number of Cuban military, forestry, and educational advisers also worked with the régime. Río Muni was used as a Cuban staging-ground for Angola. After the evacuation of their workers and embassy staff, the Nigerian government paid little attention to events in Equatorial Guinea. Other nations as varied as North Korea, Sweden, and Germany conducted trade, aid, and other business with the régime. Macías was an expert at survival on the international scene by keeping his administration flexible to foreign aid and investment. Not only did this aid keep him and his régime of terror in power for eleven years, but also, the misdirection of funds made Macías personally wealthy.

United Nations agencies said little about the situation under the Macías régime in spite of the restriction and harassment of their personnel and the interruption of their projects. The UN Development Programme (UNDP), UNESCO, WHO, FAO, and the ILO all operated or still operate in Equatorial Guinea. UNDP director Mittchel Louis of Haiti and several members of his staff were beaten after Macías accused them of complicity in a 1973 coup attempt. The Organization for African Unity provided aid to Equatorial Guinea, but refused to act on any allegations of gross human rights violations, claiming that they did not wish to interfere in their members' domestic affairs. Right-wing groups took no interest in the case and left-wing organizations actively supported Macías, seeing that his régime was surrounded with all the trappings of Marxism. Few diplomats, technicians, advisory officials, and businessmen claimed to recognize anything unusual in Equatorial Guinea even while their counterparts continued to 'commit suicide' or 'disappear' and refugees increased daily. In spite of the brutal facts and the many restrictions, few people asked questions. The GNP and exports dropped rapidly. Military expenditure was and continues to be unusually high. As many as 50,000 people may have been killed since independence. Under Macías, a protective wall of silence was built by ensuring all major powers, neighbouring nations, and potentially concerned parties had vested interests in his régime, irrespective of the terror it fostered.

Some protesting voices were eventually heard. ANRD and various human rights organizations, such as the Anti-Slavery Society and Amnesty International, pressed cases before several international bodies. In December 1978, the International Commission of Jurists accused the Macías régime of completely liquidating its opponents within Equatorial Guinea. A hard fight was eventually waged on the international front, but depressing delays allowed a régime, whose human rights record was proportionally worse than Nazi-occupied Europe, to continue unobstructed for eleven years.

Equatorial Guinea before the United Nations

It was not until 1977, after two years of deliberations that the United Nations Commission on Human Rights (UNCHR) felt that the case was worthy of examination. The Macías government rejected critics as the instruments of 'imperialism'. The UNCHR observer for Equatorial Guinea attempted to convince an unbelieving Commission that those people reportedly executed or murdered were in fact alive and in several cases working in their official roles both at home and abroad. In February 1977, the Commission decided to establish direct and confidential contacts with the régime, but this was rejected by Macías who eventually refused all contacts with the Commission. In March 1978, the Secretary-General reiterated his proposal and was again refused. The Commission received additional information concerning slavery, religious repression and penal conditions. Numerous times the Equatorial Guinean representative to the United Nations and other régime officials denied all accusations. The situation was deadlocked in spite of increasing international exposure until just before the coup when the Commission decided to abandon the use of Procedure 1503, which provided for confidential consideration of the case, and send a special rapporteur directly to Malabo to report on the situation and make public recommendations.

By the time Special Rapporteur Professor Fernando Volio Jimenez of Costa Rica went to Equatorial Guinea, the Obiang régime, which promised him unfettered access to all people and places, was well established. Beginning on 1 November 1979, the special rapporteur spent two weeks in Equatorial Guinea, visiting an amazing variety of people in both Fernando Po and Río Muni. He reported that although missions had reopened, prisoners had been released, and restored rights had promoted a feeling of relief, not all was well in Equatorial Guinea. The rapporteur was obstructed in several instances and prevented from seeing certain individuals and officials. He noted the continuation of slavery, refugee problems, and an overall absence of democratic institutions. Jimenez visited Bata Jail, but was unable to visit Malabo Jail. During his tour, the rapporteur was injured in a road accident and after this, government cooperation continued to be scarce. His numerous and detailed written queries to régime officials went unanswered. Clearly, Obiang had no interest in disclosing the whole truth.

In his report to the Commission dated 12 February 1980, Jimenez made his recommendations. Noting the lack of direction and inefficiency in the aftermath of dictatorship, he recommended an expert be sent to the Equatorial Guinean government to assist in the reconstruction of all facets of economic and socio-political life. Jimenez expressed serious criticisms of slavery, the status of women, the lack of a judicial system, and the government refusal to set a date for return to democratic civilian rule. Eventually, the Commission would choose Jimenez as their exper, but Malabo's interest in human rights would prove uninspired.

Equatorial Guinea under Obiang

After the August 1979 coup, power was transferred to a Supreme Military Council with the president having the power to rule by decree. In 1981, Obiang appointed a number of civilian cabinet members. A new and heavily criticized constitution came into effect after a referendum on 15 August 1982. The president was to be elected but with a greatly extended term of office. Under the terms of the 1982 Constitution, the president was given extensive powers, including naming and dismissing cabinet members, making decree laws, dissolving the legislature, negotiating and ratifying treaties, and calling elections. Although several former military officers have remained in the cabinet, the government assumed a more civilian character. Maintaining close supervision of military activity, Obiang has remained commander-in-chief of the armed forces and defence minister.

In mid-1983, a sixty-member unicameral 'Chamber of Representatives of the People' was formed, comprising fifteen leaders appointed by the president and forty-five members chosen by indirect elections. All adult citizens voted by secret ballot. However, the parliament is not independent and is unable to act without presidential approval.

The country was divided into seven provinces, in turn divided into districts and municipalities. The judicial system also follows these administrative levels, with the president and his advisers at the top. The current court system is a combination of traditional, civil, and military justice, and operates in an *ad hoc* manner for lack of established procedures and experienced judicial personnel, a reality which disturbs both exiles and international human rights organizations. Nor are political rights freely exercised. A single party to which all adults must pay dues, the Democratic Party for Equatorial Guinea, was formed on 30 July 1987. Many factors, such as discontent among military personnel displaced by civilians, intra-tribal and ethnic rivalries, and personal ambitions among those who regarded themselves as an alternative leadership for the country, led to three abortive coups in 1981, 1983 and 1986. These coup attempts have had little civilian or military support.

Diplomatically, Equatorial Guinea has undergone a transformation which has led to the régime's increased acceptance by the West. Equatorial Guinea's relations with the Soviet bloc have cooled considerably since 1979. The fishing treaty giving Soviet fleets access to the port of Luba was abrogated shortly after Obiang came into power. Soviet and Cuban activities in the military and economic spheres have been halted. Diplomatic recognition has been spurred on by visits from Spanish King Juan Carlos, Pope John Paul II and numerous high-ranking Spanish, French and African leaders and officials. After Macías' fall, President Obiang asked for Spanish assistance, and since then, Spain has regained some of its historical pre-eminence. Permanent agreements for economic and technical co-operation, private concessions, and trade relations have been signed. However, Spanish power in the area is rapidly being eclipsed by that of France and nearby francophone nations. Cameroon and Gabon have provided significant political and economic support to Equatorial Guinea. The latter, in turn, by joining the Central African Economic and Customs Union (UDEAC), has taken the first steps toward integration into the economy and politics of the central African region. Parallel to these developments, France has taken a greater interest in Equatorial Guinea and has augmented its aid programmes in the country. In 1984, France became Equatorial Guinea's leading trade partner, and the role of Paris has significantly increased following Equatorial Guinea's entry into the CFA franc zone and the Banque des Etats d'Afrique Centrale (BEAC). French technical advisers work in several ministries, and agreements have been signed for infrastructure development projects.

The Obiang régime is credited with restoring greater personal freedoms, reopening the schools and expanding primary education, improving public utilities and roads, as well as attracting considerable foreign aid. However, it has been criticized for not reducing petty corruption and effectively sharing power with a more representative group of Fang, Ndowe, and Bubi leaders. The current government has made very little progress in stimulating the economy, halting inflation and eliminating the black market. The well-publicized existence of modest petroleum reserves off-shore has increased expectations but generated little of substance. Extremely serious health conditions persist and the education system remains in desperate condition. The atrocities that characterized the Macías years have been eliminated, but an effective rule of law does not exist. Since 1979, Obiang has been the country's dominant political force. Described as a superstitious and brutal man, he has been constrained only by a need to maintain a consensus among his advisers and political supporters, most of whom are Fang. Obiang also appears to be willing to use African 'authenticity' in ways similar to his uncle. Religious freedom existed until early 1986 when the government closed the meeting-places of some religious denominations. In 1991 the United Nations Commission on Human Rights continued to regard the country as a high risk in light of the little progress which has been made to establish democratic and pluralistic legal and administrative institutions.

Concluding remarks

Equatorial Guinea is one of Africa's smallest nations and therefore its affairs are unlikely to arouse much interest. As Spain's only colony in black Africa, its Hispanic culture has made it an odd man out from the very beginning. Hence, few people have ever heard of the country, which is often confused with Guinea-Conakry, Guinea-Bissau or even Papua New Guinea. A substantial portion of this ignorance is also clearly the result of the unwillingness of governments, corporations and international organizations to release information. Many nations in the Western, Soviet and non-aligned blocs ignored the pleas of refugees in favour of lucrative concessions, strategic advantages or ideological considerations. Although the UN has become interested in the case, Equatorial Guinea is a living illustration of the difficulties which the international community faces in dealing with gross violations of human rights in even the smallest of nations. The scant interest in Equatorial Guinea, not only by the public and press, but also in official circles to this day, serves to underline the problem even more. Equatorial Guinea is in a devastated condition. Its case is important as a test for the UN Human Rights Commission's advisory services. Yet after almost two decades of Commission activity, few substantial reforms have been instated as a result of its decisions. The 1979 coup was a result of personal conflict in Equatorial Guinea, influenced only slightly by events in Geneva. Today Equatorial Guinea is in a state of flux. The country will probably never reach even the standard of living it had at independence. Whether any power can develop this dark corner of the African continent into a modern nation-state remains unknown.

Names and Orthography

Names and the standardization of terms are difficulties faced in conducting any research on Equatorial Guinea. However, unlike many Third World countries, place-names (even those which have been changed over the years) tend to have standardized, usually Spanish, forms. One exception to this is Fernando Po, which appears as Fernando Póo in Spanish. The name of the largest tribe in Equatorial Guinea also appears in differing forms depending on the language used by any particular author: Pangwe (German), Pamue (Spanish), Pahouin (French), Fang (English and French) and Fan (English and Spanish). I have used 'Fang' throughout.

The name 'Equatorial Guinea' is quite cumbersome. However, I felt that its use (along with 'Equatorial Guinean') was necessary to avoid confusion with the three other nations which use 'Guinea' in their names. To a Spanish readership, 'Guinea' may be sufficient, but the full usage is required elsewhere. The term 'Equatoguinean' is a recent usage for 'Equatorial Guinean', but as it is not widely accepted I have not used it.

Several place-names have changed two or three times (e.g., Fernando Po to Masie Nguema Island to Bioko). I have used the Spanish names for the sake of continuity and in recognition of the fact that most Equatorial Guineans continue to use the old forms. The only exceptions I have made are for the three cities of Malabo, Luba and Riaba, whose new names have acquired wider currency.

I would like to remind the reader that Spanish personal names consist of a given name, the father's family's name, the mother's family's name and often other names (saints, elders, etc.). Thus, for example, Fernando Volio Jimenez is referred to as Volio or Volio

Jimenez. Where numerous individuals share a common name – no fewer than thirteen Ndongos have had important roles in Equatorial Guinea's past and present – names have been lengthened to avoid confusion. Hence Atanasio Ndongo Miyone appears as Atanasio Ndongo and Ndongo Miyone, but never simply as Ndongo. Proper usage is applied regardless of press usage.

The Country and Its People

1 **Small is not beautiful: the story of Equatorial Guinea.**
Max Liniger-Goumaz. London: Hurst, 1989. 198p. bibliog.
As the outstanding specialist on Equatorial Guinea, Professor Liniger-Goumaz
provides an excellent overview of the country in this book translated from the French
by John Wood. Examined in this work are the physical and human geography of
Fernando Po, Río Muni and Annobón; European exploration, administration,
missions, education, health and the economy during the colonial era; the struggle for
and attainment of independence; demography, religion, education, health, the media
and the economy under the Nguema dictatorships; and the present conditions and
future prospects for Equatorial Guinea. Many useful statistics are also included as well
as an excellent section of bibliographical notes.

2 **Background notes on Equatorial Guinea.**
US Department of State. Washington, DC: US Government Printing
Office, March 1989. 6p.
A pamphlet for public distribution which provides general facts and figures about the
country, including material on geography, cultures, history, government, political
conditions, the economy, foreign relations, defence, US–Equatorial Guinea relations
and travel notes.

Equatorial Guinea: an African tragedy.
See item no. 63.

Guinea.
See item no. 66.

Equatorial Guinea: colonialism, state terror and the search for stability.
See item no. 175.

1

The Country and Its People

La Guinée équatoriale, un pays méconnu. (Equatorial Guinea: the mis-understood land.)
See item no. 333.

Equatorial Guinea.
See item no. 334.

Travel Guides

3 **Central Africa: a travel survival kit.**
Alex Newton. Hawthorn, Victoria, Australia: Lonely Planet, 1989.
260p. maps.

This unique travel guide covers Equatorial Guinea on pages 158 to 170. It offers a historical, cultural and geographical survey of the country. But more importantly, it dispenses practical information on climate, visa regulations, currency, health, security, business hours, communications and transport to and from the country and internally. More specific information on shopping, entertainment, sights, accommodation and dining is provided for Malabo, Luba, Bata and Ebébiyin. Maps of Equatorial Guinea and the major streets of Malabo are provided, as well as a few colour photos.

4 **Equatorial Guinea post report.**
Washington, DC: US Department of State, Oct. 1986. 12p.

Intended as a guide for American diplomats and their family members posted in Equatorial Guinea, this report truthfully and practically describes living conditions in the country in the 1980s, but without attempting any background analysis of those conditions. A number of interesting black-and-white photographs illustrate the text.

Background notes on Equatorial Guinea.
See item no. 2.

3

Explorers' and Travellers' Accounts

Early

5 **Remarks on the country extending from Cape Palmas to the river Congo.**
John Adams. London: Frank Cass, 1966. 265p.
As an early British explorer and trader on the west coast of Africa, John Adams made a total of ten voyages along that coast between 1786 and 1800. This reprint of his 1823 book, published in London, contains his records and observations of what is now Fernando Po, Río Muni and the coastal areas of adjacent countries.

6 **Narrative of the expedition sent by Her Majesty's government to the river Niger in 1841, under the command of Capt. H. D. Trotter.**
William Allen, Thomas Thompson. New York: Johnson Reprint, 1967. 2 vols.
William Allen was a British naval officer who accompanied the 1832 Lander-Oldfield expedition to the Niger and the Trotter expedition of 1841. This reprint of Allen's London original of 1848 includes an account of travels on and around Fernando Po.

7 **A new and accurate description of the coast of Guinea, divided into the Gold, the Slave and the Ivory Coasts written originally in Dutch and now faithfully done into English.**
Willem Bosman. London: Frank Cass, 1967. 577p. maps.
Originally published in London by F. Knapton in 1705, Dutch sea captain Bosman's amazing and colourful accounts include material on Fernando Po, Corisco and Annobón. The age of this work shines thorough in its much more marvelling tone compared to later accounts. This reprint is introduced by John Ralph Willis and includes maps and notes by J. D. Fage and R. E. Bradbury.

8 **Benin-Nun-Bonny River to Fernando Po.**
   Richard F. Burton.   In: J. Holpman's *Travels in Madeira, Sierra Leone,
   Teneriffe, St. Jage, Cape Coast, Fernando Po, Prince's Island, Etc.*,
   London: Routledge, 1870.

As explorer, scholar and author, Richard Francis Burton smuggled his way into the
Muslim holy city of Mecca, discovered Lake Tanganyika and thrilled the readers of his
age with both tales of adventure and painstaking scholarship. Posted in Santa Isabel as
British Consul to the Bights of Biafra and Benin from 1861 to 1864, Burton travelled
widely along the coast. This is one of many accounts of the area which he wrote.

9 **Wanderings in West Africa from Liverpool to Fernando Po.**
   Richard F. Burton.   London: Johnson Reprint, 1969. 260p.

Originally published in London by Tinsley Brothers in 1863, this collection of Burton's
accounts includes material on Fernando Po and his voyage there.

10 **A mission to Gelele, King of Dahome.**
    Richard F. Burton.   New York: Praeger, 1966. 372p.

Originally published in London by Tinsley Brothers in 1864, this is an account of one
of Burton's missions while consul in Santa Isabel, Fernando Po.

11 **Two trips to gorilla land and the cataracts of the Congo.**
    Richard F. Burton.   New York: Johnson Reprint, 1967. 355p. maps.

Originally published in London by Marston, Low & Searle in 1876, this book traces
Burton's attempts to find a gorilla (after reading the accounts of Du Chaillu). Although
his quest was unsuccessful, this work is anthropologically important as it includes his
encounters with the Fang. Two folding maps are included.

12 **Journal of the expedition to explore the course and termination of the
    Niger.**
    Richard L. Lander, John Lander.   New York: J. & J. Harper, 1832.
    2 vols.

Richard Lemon Lander, a servant of the explorer Clapperton and then explorer
himself, laid the groundwork for British influence along the Niger. For him, as for
many others, Santa Isabel was a staging-post. After being injured on a trading journey
on the Niger in 1834, Lander died in Santa Isabel and is buried not far from the city.
Accounts of and information on Fernando Po are found in vol. 2, pages 291-315.

Colonial

13 **Fernando Póo y el Muni, sus misterios, sus riquezas, su colonialización.**
(Fernando Po and the Muni: their mysteries, their riches, their
colonization.)
Juan Bravo Carbonell.   Madrid: Imprenta de Alrededor de Mundo,
1917. 399p.
In describing the Spanish colonies in the Gulf of Guinea, Juan Bravo Carbonell,
general secretary of Fernando Po's Official Agricultural Chamber and a first-rate
scholar, postulates what Spain could do with her colonies. But, as history would show,
Madrid did not listen to this visionary.

14 **Territorios españoles del Golfo de Guinea.** (Spanish territories in the Gulf
of Guinea.)
Juan Bravo Carbonell.   Madrid: Imprenta Zoila Ascasibar, 1929. 215p.
This work by Bravo Carbonell provides a good overview of pre-Franco Spanish
Guinea.

15 **Anecdotario pamue: impresiones de Guinea.** (Fang anecdotes:
impressions of Guinea.)
Juan Bravo Carbonell.   Madrid: Editora Nacional, 1942. 190p.
One of Bravo Carbonell's last works, his anecdotes fill out the scholarship of his
previous work with description and opinion.

16 **Apuntes sobre el estado de la Costa occidental de Africa y principalmente
de las posesiones españolas en el Golfo de Guinea.** (A memorandum on
the condition of the west coast of Africa and the establishment of
Spanish possessions in the Gulf of Guinea.)
Carlos Chacón.   Madrid: Imprenta Nacional, 1859. 167p.
As the first Spanish governor of Fernando Po, Carlos Chacón can be truly said to be
the founder of the Spanish colony. He arrived in May 1858 with a doctor, engineer,
Jesuits and infantry and within a few months laid the framework of the island's colonial
system. These are his memoirs.

17 **Cannibals were my friends: Finlay's true Fernandian tale.**
C. Finlay.   Evesham, England: Arthur James, 1957. 96p.
Told by J. W. Richardson, this colourful 19th-century account of Fernando Po is
exciting and humorous, but does much to perpetuate the myths and rumours
(particularly of cannibalism) rife on the west African coast.

18 **Impressions of West Africa.**
T. J. Hutchinson.   London: Longman, 1958.
As British Consul in Santa Isabel from 1855 to 1861, Hutchinson has much to say
about west Africa. Pages 173 to 202 deal with Fernando Po and provide a description
of the island in the late 1850s.

19   **Africa: viajes y trabajos de la asociación euskara La Exploradora.**
(Africa: journeys and labours of the Exploradora Society.)
Manuel Iradier y Bulfy.   Vitoria, Spain: de Iturbe, 1887, 1901. 2 vols.
maps.

Manuel Iradier was Spain's answer to France's De Brazza, Germany's Nachtigal and Britain's Burton and Speke. He has often been called the 'Spanish Stanley', though apart from the acquisition of territory for European powers the two men had little in common. As the man whose tireless energy insured Spanish presence on the African mainland in Río Muni, Iradier took copious notes and collected numerous souvenirs. In this two-volume set in Spanish, Iradier describes in detail the exploration and acquisition of Río Muni and the additional territories which Spain later lost as a result of the Berlin Conference of 1885. Volume I deals with Iradier's exploration from 1875 to 1877 and Volume II with Iradier's journey to acquire large areas of the mainland for Spain in 1884. Illustrations, maps and music are included. This work was also reprinted by the Consejo de Cultura de la Excelentísima Diputación Foral de Alava in 1958.

20   **Travels in West Africa: Congo Français, Corisco and Cameroons.**
Mary H. Kingsley.   London: Macmillan, 1897. 741p.

Mary Kingsley, a remarkable English women who went along the Atlantic coast of Africa as a palm oil trader in the early 1890s, spent a significant amount of her time on Fernando Po and in the Fang country of present-day Equatorial Guinea, Gabon and Cameroon. Her descriptions of people, places, flora and fauna are vivid and full of wit. More than any other early traveller in Africa, she had an understanding curiosity about and love for the black African. It is not surprising that she devoted large portions of this work to the customs, coinage, dances, histories, rumours, apparel, agriculture, attitudes, crafts and other descriptions of the Bubi of Fernando Po and the Fang. Numerous illustrations and photographs are included. Valuable appendices document trade and labour problems, diseases, reptiles, fish, insects, shells, plants and the cloth loom.

21   **West African studies.**
Mary H. Kingsley.   London: Macmillan, 1899. 639p.

Though second in importance to *Travels in West Africa*, this book by Kingsley fills in a good many details of west Africa and life and trade around the Gulf of Guinea. Pages 75 to 80 provide a description of Fernando Po. Appendices provide lists of trade goods, and John Harford's description of his voyage to the 'Oil Rivers' in the early 1870s. Illustrations are included.

22   **Adventures and observations on the west coast of Africa and its islands.**
Charles W. Thomas.   New York: Negro Universities Press, 1969. 479p.

Written by the chaplain to the United States Navy's 1855-57 African Squadron, Chapter 23 of this offbeat but important account deals solely with Fernando Po, São Tome and Príncipe, Annobón and the islands off Río Muni. Thomas describes the scenery, inhabitants, the port of Clarence, explorer Lander's grave and relations between Britain and Spain vis-à-vis Fernando Po. Being anti-Catholic he is particularly concerned with the religious situation – the expulsion of Protestant missionaries. This edition is a reprint of the 1860 original.

Los confinados a Fernando Póo e impresiones de un viaje a Guinea. (The exiles to Fernando Po and impressions of a journey to Guinea.)
See item no. 87.

Eine Afrikanische Tropen-insel Fernando Poo. (A tropical African island: Fernando Po.)
See item no. 88.

En el país de los Pamues. (In the land of the Fangs.)
See item no. 111.

En el país de los Bubis. (In the land of the Bubis.)
See item no. 112.

Beiträge zur Kenntniss der Bubisprache auf Fernando Poo. (Contributions to the knowledge of the Bubi language of Fernando Po.)
See item no. 123.

Corisco days: the first thirty years of the West African Mission.
See item no. 155.

Post-colonial

23 **Tropical gangsters.**
Robert Klitgaard. New York: Basic Books, 1990. 281p.
Residing in Equatorial Guinea during the late 1980s, Klitgaard was an official of the World Bank who administered a programme aimed at rebuilding the crumbled economic and financial institutions of the country. This work is written as a traveller's account and as such is highly readable. Within this framework, Klitgaard offers many thoughtful insights into conditions in Equatorial Guinea; banking, financial and developmental institutions; the frustrations of administration and reform; the usefulness of foreign aid; dependence on foreign aid; and daily life in Equatorial Guinea in the 1980s.

24 **Aekvatorialguinea.** (Equatorial Guinea.)
E. Nilsson. *KD* (Copenhagen), 10, 11 and 14 March 1978.
In early 1978 Danish journalist Nilsson briefly visited Equatorial Guinea. Suspected of spying by the Macías régime, she was sheltered by a Spanish teacher in Bata and escaped to Cameroon. The above Danish-language articles on her trip and her observations of the situation in Equatorial Guinea were sub-titled 'Bevolkning er måske halveret' [The population is halved], 'Alt er forbud' [All is forbidden] and 'En fremmed på vej' [A foreigner on the road] respectively.

Equatorial Guinea – Macías country: the forgotten refugees.
See item no. 174.

Geography

25 *Calypso* explores an undersea canyon.
Jacques-Yves Cousteau. *National Geographic* (Washington, DC), March 1958, p. 373-6.
Famous oceanographer Cousteau writes of his exploration of the Romanche Trench off Annobón in this British magazine article with photographs by Bates Littlehales and Harold Edgerton.

26 Plazas y provincias africanas españolas. (Spanish African towns and provinces.)
J. Díaz de Villegas y Bustamente.   Madrid: Instituto de Estudios Africanos, 1962. 261p.
A staunch supporter of Franco, General José Díaz de Villegas y Bustamente was simultaneously director of the Dirección General de Marruecos y Colonias (Spanish Colonial Office) and the Instituto de Estudios Africanos (Institute of African Studies) from the end of the Second World War to Equatorial Guinean independence in 1968. He more than anyone else shaped the country by resisting the forces of reform and ruling with paternalistic authoritarianism. This work describes all of Spain's African colonies during the period when they were provinces of Spain (1960-64).

27 Africa and the islands.
R. J. Harrison Church.   New York: John Wiley, 1977. 542p. bibliog.
Harrison Church provides brief but good physical descriptions of Fernando Po, Annobón and Río Muni in his chapter on 'Regional Studies – Western Central Africa'.

28 Atlas histórico y geográfico de Africa española. (A historical and geographical atlas of Spanish Africa.)
Madrid: Instituto de Estudios Africanos, 1951. 203p. maps.
This official publication of the Spanish Institute of African Studies provides forty-seven maps and twenty drawings of Spain's African territories (Morocco, the Spanish Sahara, the Canaries and Spanish Guinea). Sections on various aspects of the geography and

9

history of these territories are written from an official Spanish perspective. In all, 6,000 geographical locations and historical names are mentioned, described and/or located.

29 Change in place names.
Keesing's Contemporary Archives (London), 21-27 Jan. 1974, p. 26308.

In 1973, the Macías régime 'Africanized' all place-names. Santa Isabel became Malabo, San Carlos became Luba, Concepción became Riaba, Fernando Po became Francisco Macías Nguema Island (later Masie Nguema Island), Rio Muni became Mbini, etc. (only the first three of these have been widely accepted). This entry in *Keesing's Contemporary Archives* explains the changes.

30 Geografía de Guinea Ecuatorial. (A geography of Equatorial Guinea.)
Madrid: Ministry of National Education, 1985.

As a general geographical survey, this recent text offers a good first approach to the country.

31 Notas geográficas, físicas y económicas sobre los territorios españoles del Golfo de Guinea. (Geographical, physical and economic notes on the Spanish territories in the Gulf of Guinea.)
Jaime Nosti Nava. Madrid: Talleres Tipográficos Espasa-Calpe, 1942. 116p. maps. bibliog.

This geographical study intended primarily as a reference work for agriculture is the first in a series of monographs sponsored by the Dirección de Agricultura de los Territorios Españoles del Golfo de Guinea. But Nosti Nava, head of the Dirección de Agricultura from 1940 to 1960, goes well beyond mere description and offers plans and suggestions for how the country could be improved. Folding colour maps, colour plates and other illustrations enhance this excellent work of scholarship by the most renowned Spanish expert on agriculture in what is now Equatorial Guinea.

32 A comprehensive geography of west Africa.
Reuben K. Udo. New York: Africana, 1978. 304p. maps. bibliog.

This well-illustrated general geography is based on a division of the African continent which places Fernando Po, but not Río Muni within 'West Africa'. Hence only the island part of Equatorial Guinea is covered in this work. Chapter 17 – Fernando Po – includes information on relief and drainage; climate, vegetation and soils; economic activities; population and settlement, transportation and foreign trade. Information, often based on colonial era sources, can be a bit dated. Three unique and useful maps within the chapter offer much information on relief, export crops and agricultural land use.

33 Geografía e historia de la Guinea Española. (A geography and history of Spanish Guinea.)
Tomas L. Pujadas, Manuel Pérez. Madrid: Instituto de Estudios Africanos, 1959. 112p.

As in the writings of Jaime Nosti Nava, Pujadas' and Pérez's description includes prescriptions on how Equatorial Guinea could be developed. In 1969 this work was updated as *Geografía e historia de la Guinea Ecuatorial* and published by the Catholic Mission in Santa Isabel. However, the newer edition is more difficult to find. Along with Nosti Nava's work, this book provides a good survey of the country, much of which remains current.

34 **Sintesis geográfica de Fernando Póo.** (Geographical synthesis of Fernando Po.)
Manuel de Teran.   Madrid: Instituto de Estudios Africanos, 1962. 116p. maps.

A good, but brief, geography of Fernando Po.

Small is not beautiful: the story of Equatorial Guinea.
See item no. 1.

Background notes on Equatorial Guinea.
See item no. 2.

Presença do arquipelago de São Tomé e Príncipe na moderna cultural portuguesa. (The presence of the archipelago of São Tomé and Príncipe in modern Portuguese culture.)
See item no. 56.

Equatorial Guinea: an African tragedy.
See item no. 63.

Historia geográfica de la isla de Fernando Póo. (A geographical history of the island of Fernando Po.)
See item no. 94.

Guinea Continental Española. (Continental Spanish Guinea.)
See item no. 95.

Annobón: l'île oubliée. (Annobón: the forgotten island.)
See item no. 96.

Islas del Golfo de Guinea. (Islands of the Gulf of Guinea.)
See item no. 97.

Notícia de Annobón: su geografía, historia y costumbres. (News of Annobón: its geography, history and customs.)
See item no. 98.

African boundaries: a legal and diplomatic encyclopedia.
See item no. 214.

La Guinée équatoriale, un pays méconnu. (Equatorial Guinea: the misunderstood land.)
See item no. 333.

Equatorial Guinea.
See item no. 334.

Geology

35 **Datos geomorfológicos de la Guinea Continental Española.**
(Geomorphological facts of continental Spanish Guinea.)
Manuel Alia Medina.   Madrid: Instituto de Estudios Africanos, 1951.
63p. maps. bibliog.
This collection of information and maps has remained the most important work on the geology of Equatorial Guinea.

36 **Informe al gobierno de la República de Guinea Ecuatorial referente a política minera y petrolera.** (A report to the government of the Republic of Equatorial Guinea relating to mineral and petroleum policy.)
R. Arce.   Santa Isabel: United Nations Development Programme, 1971.
This UN report reviews the potential resources and possible plans for the development of mineral and petroleum industries in the country.

37 **Estudio petrográfico de la Guinea Continental Española.** (A petrographic study of continental Spanish Guinea.)
José M. Fuster Casas.   Madrid: Instituto de Estudios Africanos, 1951.
355p. maps. bibliog.
As the first scientist to conduct a petrographic study of Río Muni, Fuster Casas provides the basis for more recent research by others (see item no. 38). Colour plates included.

38 **Equatorial Guinea: annual review 1984.**
Petroconsultants, SA.   Geneva: International Energy Service of
Petroconsultants, SA, Jan. 1985. 13p. map.

A petroleum industry consultant's summary of petroleum potential in the country
illustrated with a 1:1,000,000 map. These annual reviews have continued to provide the
most up-to-date research information on petroleum and the petroleum industry in
Equatorial Guinea.

**Excelente calidad del petróleo de Guinea Ecuatorial, según los estudios de la
empresa mixta Gepsa.** (The excellent quality of Equatorial Guinean
petroleum, according to the studies of the mixed enterprise GEPSA.)
See item no. 249.

Flora and Fauna

39 **Flore du Gabon.** (Flora of Gabon.)
A. Aubreville. Paris: Musée National d'Histoire Naturelle, 1961-73.
23 vols.
This exhaustive botanical work on Gabon is useful for the plants of neighbouring Río Muni.

40 **Aves de la isla de Fernando Póo.** (Birds of the island of Fernando Po.)
A. Basilio. Madrid: Editorial Co. SA, 1963.
Basilio's work on the birds of Fernando Po remains the principal work on the subject.

41 **La vida animal en la Guinea española.** (Animal life in Spanish Guinea.)
A. Basilio. Madrid: Instituto de Estudios Africanos, 1962. 190p. map.
This general presentation of animal life in Equatorial Guinea remains the best general work on the fauna of Equatorial Guinea. It contains numerous illustrations.

42 **Catálogo descriptivo de los mamíferos de la Guinea española.**
(A descriptive catalogue of the mammals of Spanish Guinea.)
A. Cabrera. *Memoria* (Real Sociedad Española de Historia Natural, Madrid), vol. XVI, no. 1 (1929).
In spite of being short, Cabrera's article adds much to the study of the large variety of mammals in the region.

43 **Tingidos de la Guinea española.** (Lace bugs of Spanish Guinea.)
Juan Gómez-Menor Ortega. Madrid: Instituto de Estudios Africanos, 1955. 46p.
A specialized illustrated study on lace bugs, an insect pest which destroys foliage as a result of feeding on its juices.

44 **Ensayo geobotánico de la Guinea continental española.** (A geo-botanical essay on continental Spanish Guinea.)
E. Guinea López. Madrid: Dirección de Agricultura, 1946. 338p. bibliog.

Emilio Guinea López was the leading authority on the flora of Río Muni and this old but accurate work still remains the principal study on this topic.

45 **A comparative ecology of *Gorilla gorilla* and *Pantroglodytes* in Río Muni, West Africa.**
Clyde Jones, Jorge Sabater Pi. Basel; New York: S. Karger, 1971. 96p. maps. bibliog.

It was in the region comprising present-day Río Muni, Gabon and the Congo Republic that Europeans and hence modern scientists made their first contact with the gorilla. This short scholarly work on gorillas and other primates in Río Muni provides some of the most recent nature studies of the area. Illustrations are included. See also item no. 47.

46 **Projecto de investigación y conservación de la naturaleza en Guinea Ecuatorial.** (A nature conservation and investigation project in Equatorial Guinea.)
Malabo: Oficina de Cooperación con Guinea Ecuatorial, 1986. 29p.

An illustrated booklet by the foreign aid office of the Spanish Foreign Ministry describing the latest efforts in natural conservation in the country.

47 **Snowflake: the world's first white gorilla.**
Arthur Riopelle (text), Paul Zahl (photography). *National Geographic* (Washington, DC), vol. CXXXI, no. 3 (March 1967), p. 442-8.

The discovery of an albino gorilla in the forests of Río Muni in the mid-1960s brought the country to the attention of naturalists worldwide. This article traces the work of Tulane University researcher Riopelle and Spanish naturalist Jorge Sabater Pi in describing the African setting of this rare find and the gorilla's eventual transfer to Barcelona Zoo. At that time some 5,000 little-studied lowland gorillas were believed to inhabit Río Muni's forests. Excellent photography is included. See also item no. 45.

48 **Peces de Río Muni.** (Fishes of Río Muni.)
Benigno Román Roig. Badalona, Spain: Fundación 'la Salle' de Ciencias Naturales, 1971. 295p.

An illustrated guide to the fishes of Río Muni, sponsored by the Instituto de Estudios Africanos.

Travels in West Africa: Congo Français, Corisco and Cameroons.
See item no. 20.

En el país de los Pamues. (In the land of the Fangs.)
See item no. 111.

Flora and Fauna

En el país de los Bubis. (In the land of the Bubis.)
See item no. 112.

El bosque de la Guinea: exploración y explotación. (The forests of Guinea: exploration and exploitation.)
See item no. 262.

Estudio sobre la constitución y explotación del bosque en la Guinea Continental Española. (A study of the constitution and exploitation of the forests of continental Spanish Guinea.)
See item no. 263.

Situation forestière en Guinée Equatoriale. (The forestry situation in Equatorial Guinea.)
See item no. 265.

Prehistory and Archaeology

49 **Grinding benches and mortars on Fernando Po.**
R. A. Kennedy. *Man*, vol. LXII (Sept. 1962). p. 129-30.
This specialized work is one of a very few in English on archaeological finds on Fernando Po.

50 **Fernando Po and Gabon.**
P. De Maret. In: *The Archaeology of Central Africa*, Graz, Austria: Akademische Druck- u. Verlagsanstalt, 1982.
A general work offering some material on archaeological finds, and interpretations and studies on the prehistory of Equatorial Guinea.

51 **Etapas de la cultura carboneras de Fernando Póo en el primer milenio de nuestra era.** (Stages of the Carboneras culture of Fernando Po in the first millennium of our era.)
Amador Martín del Molino. Madrid: Instituto de Estudios Africanos, 1968. 33p. bibliog.
As no. 18 in the IEA's African monograph series, this booklet lays down the chronological divisions of the Carboneras culture of Fernando Po (Boloapi I, Boloapi Boloapi II and Buela). This system has remained in use to the present day.

52 **La prehistoria de Fernando Póo.** (The prehistory of Fernando Po.)
Augusto Panyella-Gómez. *Archivos del Instituto de Estudios Africanos* (Madrid), no. 49 (1959), p. 3-21.
Panyella-Gómez was one of Spain's leading archaeologist/anthropologists and this piece provides an overview of Fernando Po's prehistory which has been frequently added to by other scholars and by Panyella-Gómez himself.

17

53 **Primeros resultados de la campaña de excavaciones del I.E.A. en Fernando Póo.** (First results of the I.E.A. Excavation Campaign on Fernando Po.)
Augusto Panyella-Gómez. *Archivos del Instituto de Estudios Africanos* (Madrid), no. 62 (1962).

This is the best of many preliminary reports issued by Panyella-Gómez on his findings on Fernando Po.

54 **Prehistoria de Río Muni.** (A prehistory of Río Muni.)
R. Perramón Marti. *Guinea Española* (Madrid), vol. LXIII, nos 1606, 1607 and 1609 (Sept., Oct. and Dec. 1966), p. 195-200, 224-30 and 298-305.

Material on the prehistory of Río Muni is difficult to find and often bears the name of Perramón Marti. This is a three-part magazine article on the prehistory of Río Muni which followed a shorter, earlier (May 1966) article in *Guinea Española.*

55 **Contribución a la prehistoria y protohistoria de Río Muni.** (A contribution to the prehistory and protohistory of Río Muni.)
R. Perramón Marti. Santa Isabel: Instituto Claretiano de Africanistas, 1968. 20p. bibliog.

This important, but difficult to find, publication of the Claretian Institute of Africanists is the most outstanding archaeological work on Río Muni.

History

Africa and west and equatorial Africa

56 **Presença do arquipelago de São Tomé e Príncipe na moderna cultural portuguesa.** (The presence of the archipelago of São Tomé and Príncipe in modern Portuguese culture.)
Cesar Amandio. São Tomé, 1968.
This major work in Portuguese examines the role of Portugal in Africa and the influences which passed between Lisbon's African colonial empire and its European motherland. It includes material on Portuguese rule and influences in what is now Equatorial Guinea.

57 **White man's grave: the story of the west African coast.**
. L. G. Green. London: Stanley Paul, 1954.
Until improvements in medicine and sanitation in the 20th century, the coasts along the Gulf of Guinea were known by a variety of nicknames, usually referring to the unhealthy state of the region. Among these are 'death's waiting room' and 'the white man's grave'. Much stamina and courage was required of those Europeans who ventured on to the west African coast. This general history is the story of European influence in west Africa and as such it provides an excellent backdrop to the early history of Fernando Po and other islands and territories in the Gulf of Guinea.

58 **A history of the colonization of Africa by alien races.**
Harry H. Johnston. London: Cambridge University Press, 1899. 505p.
In the course of documenting the colonization of Africa, H. H. Johnston, who was also the British consul in Santa Isabel from 1887 to 1888, records his observations on Spain's colonies on pages 116 to 122.

59 **George Grenfell and the Congo.**
Harry H. Johnston. New York: D. Appleton, 1910. 2 vols, 990p.
Although not primarily on Spanish Guinea, this lengthy book provides a great deal of information on the Spanish colonies throughout pages 882 to 962, including notes on the Bubi language, the Fang, and the geography, animals and people of Fernando Po.

60 **The northern Gabon coast to 1875.**
K. David Patterson. Oxford: Clarendon Press, 1975. 167p.
In describing the origins of Gabon, Patterson frequently alludes to Corisco Island, the Muni estuary and personalities (Burton, Nassau, and others) significant in the early colonial history of Fernando Po and Río Muni.

61 **Germans in the Cameroons 1884-1914.**
Harry Rudin. New York: Greenwood, 1968. 456p.
Described as a case-study in modern imperialism, this reprint of the Yale University Press original of 1938 offers an excellent history of German influence and colonialism in the Cameroons and the Gulf of Guinea until 1914. However, one wishes that Rudin had continued his study through to the aftermath of the First World War. Relations with the Spanish, border demarcations and German commercial interests which were also active in Spanish Guinea are dealt with in some detail.

62 **German imperialism in Africa.**
Edited by Helmuth Stoecker. London: Hurst, 1986. 446p.
This East German work (translated into English by Bernd Zöllner), covering German influences and imperialism in Africa from 1884 to 1945, adds details and a unique perspective to German colonialism in Cameroon, the German firms operating in Africa (including those active in Fernando Po and Río Muni) and German–Spanish colonial relations.

Travels in West Africa: Congo Français, Corisco and Cameroons.
See item no. 20.

A voyager out.
See item no. 320.

Equatorial Guinea

63 **Equatorial Guinea: an African tragedy.**
Randall Fegley. New York: Peter Lang, 1989. 310p. maps. bibliog.
This full-length history of Equatorial Guinea spans the periods from 1470 to 1989 and includes sections on early travellers to Fernando Po and Río Muni, Spanish colonialism, the struggle for independence, the politics of independence, the early post-independence period, the Macías era, human rights violations, exile politics, the overthrow of Macías, Equatorial Guinea before the UN Human Rights Commission and the country under Obiang. Many facts, figures and geographical, cultural and

biographical details are included. Appendices provide maps of the country, a glossary of abbreviations and acronyms, a list of colonial administrators and a list of the victims of the Macías régime.

64 **Historia y tragedia de Guinea Ecuatorial.** (The history and tragedy of Equatorial Guinea.)
Donato Ndongo Bidiyogo. Madrid: Cambio 16, 1977. 307p.
Although somewhat hispanocentric, this was the first full-length history of Equatorial Guinea by a national. Ndongo Bidiyogo, a member of the exile organization Alianza Nacional de Restauración Democratica, records the events of the colonial and post-colonial eras as an explanation of the terror which gripped the country under Macías.

Small is not beautiful: the story of Equatorial Guinea.
See item no. 1.

La décolonisation de la Guinée Equatoriale et le problème des réfugies. (The decolonization of Equatorial Guinea and the refugee problem.)
See item no. 172.

Equatorial Guinea: colonialism, state terror and the search for stability.
See item no. 175.

La Guinée équatoriale, un pays méconnu. (Equatorial Guinea: the misunderstood land.)
See item no. 333.

Equatorial Guinea.
See item no. 334.

Colonial

65 **Reivindicaciones de España.** (Vindications of Spain.)
José Maria de Areilza, Fernando Maria Castiella y Maiz. Madrid: Instituto de Estudios Africanos, 1941.
As Spanish Foreign Minister under the Falangist governments of Luis Carrero Blanco, Fernando Maria Castiella y Maiz's long term in office saw Equatorial Guinea change from a quiet colony to a troubled young nation. In this early tract, Castiella seeks to justify Spain's presence in Africa.

66 **Guinea.**
Luis Báguena Corella. Madrid: Instituto de Estudios Africanos, 1950. 160p.
First in a series of manuals on Spanish Africa, this Spanish-language book provides a general look at the history, geography, cultures and administration of Spanish Guinea. Seventy-six illustrations are included.

67 **Spanish Guinea: enclave empire.**
Sanford Berman. *Phylon* (The Atlanta University Review of Race and Culture), vol. XVII, no. 4. (1956), p. 349-64.
Berman provides an good overview of Spanish Guinea's history, geography, people, education, health and transport in this article, but it is his discussion of the policies and practices of the Spanish colonial administration and of Spanish motives in retaining their colonies which contribute the most to understanding Equatorial Guinea during the colonial era.

68 **El brigadier Conde de Argelejos y su expedición militar á Fernando Póo en 1778.** (Brigadier Count de Argelejos and his military expedition to Fernando Po in 1778.)
Manuel Cencillo de Pineda.   Madrid: Instituto de Estudios Africanos, 1948. 221p. maps. bibliog.
In 1778, Brigadier Felipe José, Count of Argelejos de Santos y Freire set out from Uruguay to take possession of Fernando Po and the other territories given to Spain by Portugal in the El Pardo Treaty earlier that year. The Count died and his fever-decimated crew mutinied and were imprisoned by the Portuguese on São Tomé. Only twenty-six of 150 men returned to Montevideo and they were in irons. This disastrous undertaking is frequently cited as the reason why the Spanish ignored their African possessions for another eighty years. This book in Spanish commemorates the 170th anniversary of the expedition.

69 **The impact of the Spanish Civil War and the Second World War on Portuguese and Spanish Africa.**
Gervase Clarence-Smith. *Journal of African History*, vol. XXVI (1985), p. 309-26.
From September to November 1936, a minuscule phase of the Spanish Civil War was fought on Fernando Po and in Río Muni after Franco dispatched troops from the Canary Islands to crush the socialist Frente Popular, led by Governor General Sanchez Guerra Saez and Vice-Governor General Porcel. This article examines the overall situation and its effects.

70 **Angel Barrera y las posesiones españolas del Golfo de Guinea.** (Angel Barrera and the Spanish possessions in the Gulf of Guinea.)
Manuel Góngora Echenique.   Madrid: San Bernando, 1923.
Angel Barrera y Luyando was a naval officer and Governor General of Spanish Guinea from 1910 to 1918. Concerned mainly with maintaining Fernando Po's labour supply, his administration was marked by paternalism and strong pro-German sympathies which manifested themselves in arms smuggling during the First World War and the acceptance of 60,000 refugees from German Kamerun after the war. This book is a review of his career.

71 **Opúsculo sobre la colonización de Fernando Póo y revista de los principales establecimientos europeos en la costa occidental de Africa.** (A tract on the colonization of Fernando Po and a review of the principal European establishments on the west coast of Africa.)
A. Guillemar de Aragón. Madrid: Imprenta Nacional, 1852. 152p.

On a forty-day mission from Freetown to Fernando Po and Río Muni, Adolfo Guillemar de Aragón, Spanish consul in Sierra Leone, reaffirmed Spain's claim to her territories and replaced English place-names with Spanish ones. This work in Spanish is his report and observations.

72 **Spain and the scramble for Africa: the 'Africanistas' and the Gulf of Guinea.**
Billy Gene Hahs. Unpublished thesis, University of New Mexico, Albuquerque, 1980.

As a latecomer in the scramble for African colonies, Spain proved to be the least successful European power in Africa. This thesis offers a commentary on the situation in which the Spanish found themselves in the late 19th century.

73 **Spanish Guinea: Spain's last tropical territory.**
R. J. Harrison Church. *West Africa* (London), 1960, p. 519-25.

This article looks at the situation in Spanish Guinea, the last remnant of Spain's once vast tropical empire, at a time when the rest of Africa was gaining independence.

74 **Reseña histórica de la presencia española en el Golfo de Guinea.**
(Historical notes on the Spanish presence in the Gulf of Guinea.)
José Antonio Moreno Moreno. Madrid: Instituto de Estudios Africanos, 1952. 101p.

This is a general work on Spanish colonialism in Fernando Po and Río Muni. Twenty-two illustrations are provided.

75 **Spain changes course in Africa.**
René Pélissier. *Africa Report* (New York), vol. VIII, no. 12 (Dec. 1963), p. 8-11.

A leading Equatorial Guinea expert, René Pélissier discusses the approach of autonomy in Equatorial Guinea.

76 **Uncertainty in Spanish Guinea.**
René Pélissier. *Africa Report* (New York), vol. XIII, no. 3 (March 1968), p. 16-38.

Pélissier reports on the political disagreements and party politics of Equatorial Guinea in the run-up to independence.

77 **De colonización y economía en la Guinea española.** (Concerning colonization and economics in Spanish Guinea.)
R. Perpiñá Grau. Barcelona, Spain: Editorial Labor SA, 1945. 422p. bibliog.

This is the best and most interesting presentation of the colonial system and colonial economy of Spanish Guinea as conditions were prior to the first signs of anti-colonial protest.

78 **Spain in equatorial Africa.**
Madrid: Servicio Informativo Español, 1964. 91p. maps.

This booklet is an English translation of the Spanish Information Service's *España en el Africa Ecuatorial*, which offers an official view of Spain's presence in what is now Equatorial Guinea. Illustrations are included.

Fernando Póo y el Muni, sus misterios, sus riquezas, su colonialización. (Fernando Po and the Muni: their mysteries, their riches, their colonization.)
See item no. 13.

Territorios españoles del Golfo de Guinea. (Spanish territories in the Gulf of Guinea.)
See item no. 14.

Anecdotario pamue: impresiones de Guinea. (Fang anecdotes: impressions of Guinea.)
See item no. 15.

Atlas histórico y geográfico de Africa española. (A historical and geographical atlas of Spanish Africa.)
See item no. 28.

Geografía e historia de la Guinea Española. (A geography and history of Spanish Guinea.)
See item no. 33.

Report of the International Commission of Inquiry into the existence of slavery and forced labor in the Republic of Liberia.
See item no. 93.

Historia geográfica de la isla de Fernando Póo. (A geographical history of the island of Fernando Po.)
See item no. 94.

Guinea Continental Española. (Continental Spanish Guinea.)
See item no. 95.

Islas del Golfo de Guinea. (Islands of the Gulf of Guinea.)
See item no. 97.

The Gabon and Corisco Missions.
See item no. 154.

Political movements in Spanish Guinea.
See item no. 180.

Yankee traders, old coasters and African middlemen.
See item no. 247.

Spanish Guinea.
See item no. 328.

Post-colonial

79 **Un tigre de papel.** (A paper tiger.)
Cambio 16 (Madrid), no. 409 (7 Oct. 1979), p. 58-9.
This short magazine article, accompanied by some unique photographs, describes the 1979 trial of Macías.

80 **The birth of Equatorial Guinea.**
J. A. Chandler. *Journal of African History*, no. 11 (1970), p. 464-7.
Chandler offers a brief historical description of Equatorial Guinea around the time of independence.

81 **Guinea: materia reservada.** (Guinea: reserved material.)
Rafael Fernández.   Madrid: Sedmay, 1976. 176p.
One of the first full-length commentaries in Spanish on the human rights violations of the Macías régime and the Spanish attempts to suppress the story.

82 **Guinea: Macías, la ley del silencio.** (Guinea: Macías, the rule of silence.)
R. García Domínguez.   Barcelona, Spain: Plaza y Janes, 1977. 286p.
Another attempt by a Spanish author to break the silence surrounding the case of Equatorial Guinea under Macías. A few illustrations are included.

83 **Guinea, la gran juerga negra.** (Guinea, the big, black carousel.)
Gonzalo Lara.   *Actual* (Madrid), no. 67 (1 July 1983), p. 56-63.
An impressionistic and somewhat racist look at business, government and corruption in Equatorial Guinea under Obiang. Good photographs and a chart of business relationships are included.

84 **Equatorial Guinea: a new republic.**
Rene Pélissier.   *Geographical Magazine* (London), Nov. 1968.
This general magazine article by Pélissier takes a general look at newly independent Equatorial Guinea.

85 **The real dogs of war.**
The Sunday Times (London), 16 April 1978, p. 17.
An investigative article on the unsuccessful December 1972–January 1973 plot by author Frederick Forsyth and European mercenaries to overthrow Macías. This story was also reported in *Jeune Afrique* (Paris: no. 904, 3 May 1978). See also item no. 281.

86 **Prelude to scandal.**
Ibrahim K. Sundiata. *Journal of African History*, vol. XV, no. 1 (1974), p. 97-112.
Africanist Ibrahim Sundiata describes the background to the abuses and atrocities of the Macías régime.

Equatorial Guinea – Macías country: the forgotten refugees.
See item no. 174.

Psychoses of power: African personal dictatorships.
See item no. 181.

Personal rule in black Africa.
See item no. 183.

Autopsy of a miracle.
See item no. 187.

The trial of Macías in Equatorial Guinea – the story of a dictatorship.
See item no. 190.

Military trials and the use of the death penalty in Equatorial Guinea.
See item no. 198.

Equatorial Guinea: the forgotten dictatorship.
See item no. 199.

Toda la verdad: mi intervención en Guinea. (All the truth: my intervention in Guinea.)
See item no. 321.

Fernando Po

87 **Los confinados a Fernando Póo e impresiones de un viaje a Guinea.** (The exiles to Fernando Po and impressions of a journey to Guinea.)
J. Balmesada.   Havana: Antonio Martín Lamy, 1899. 260p.
In one of many attempts to populate their African possessions the Spanish used Fernando Po as a penal colony for Cuban revolutionaries. This is a Catholic priest's account of the exiles, their journey to Fernando Po and conditions in the colony.

88 **Eine Afrikanische Tropen-insel Fernando Poo.** (A tropical African island: Fernando Po.)
Oskar Baumann.   Vienna: Edward Hölzer, 1888. 150p. bibliog.
The works of Oskar Baumann were widely acclaimed and none of his readers regarded him more highly than Mary Kingsley who frequently quotes him as a source. His observations include physical and historical descriptions of the island and information on its people ranging from data on the Bubis from drinking habits and dances to religion and language.

89 **Fernando Po and the anti-Sierra Leonean campaign 1826-1834.**
Robert Brown.   *International Journal of African Historical Studies*, vol. VI, no. 2 (1973), p. 249-64.
Fernando Po played an important role in the British anti-slavery naval patrols of the first half of the 19th century. This article examines the first phase of these operations.

90 **La colonización penitenciara de las Marianas y Fernando Póo.** (The penal colonization of the Marianas and Fernando Po.)
Francisco Lastres y Ruiz.   Madrid: E. Martínez, 1878. 68p.
The settlement of Fernando Po brought Catalan planters and Spanish colonists uprooted from Morocco to the island. But some arrivals in Santa Isabel were not willing colonists. Throughout the mid-19th century revolutionaries from Cuba and Jews unwanted in Spain were transported to Fernando Po. Written around the time when the practice was being abandoned, this is an account of the penal colonization of the island and of the Marianas in the Pacific.

91 **Historia de las ascensiones del Pico de Santa Isabel.** (A history of the ascensions of the Pico de Santa Isabel.)
J. A. Moreno Moreno.   Madrid: Instituto de Estudios Africanos, 1952. 42p. maps.
White travellers to Fernando Po and numerous famous European residents of Santa Isabel (Beecroft, Burton, Kingsley, Bravo Carbonell, and others) frequently retreated to the island's cooler and healthier highlands. Some of these Europeans climbed the Pico de Santa Isabel, which overlooks the capital. This small book with twenty-one illustrations records the various climbing excursions which took place in the first ninety years of Spanish colonial rule.

92 **The Fernandinos: labor and community in Santa Isabel de Fernando Po, 1827-1931.**
Ibrahim K. Sundiata. Unpublished thesis, Northwestern University, Evanston, Illinois, 1972. 379p.
The Fernandinos are an ethnic community, numbering some 3,500, descended from freed slaves landed by the British in the first half of the 19th century and currently found in the towns of Fernando Po. Originally from Sierra Leone, Liberia and Nigeria and frequently rescued from slavers at sea, the Fernandinos quickly adapted to Fernando Po where they became landowners, professionals, and the island's merchant class. Favoured by the Spanish, the Fernandinos were the first Africans to be allowed to enter the politics and administration of the colony. Educated, literate, wealthy and dynamic, they were particularly targeted for persecution by the Macías régime.

History. Fernando Po

Ibrahim Sundiata's PhD thesis describes the century-long story of the Fernandinos rise from being unrelated groups of impoverished ex-slaves to establishing themselves as the island's tightly knit merchant élite.

93 **Report of the International Commission of Inquiry into the existence of slavery and forced labor in the Republic of Liberia.**
Washington: US Department of State, 1931. 227p. (Publication no. 147).
For decades the labour-starved plantations of Fernando Po found a cheap and plentiful workforce in the crowded southern counties of Liberia. In 1927, the defeated candidate in Liberia's presidential election, Thomas Faulkner, accused the Liberian government of C. B. D. King of election irregularities and of condoning the recruitment of Liberians for forced labour on Fernando Po. A League of Nations investigation followed which produced this report. The commission of inquiry, composed of a former Liberian president, a Scot and a black American, found that labourers had been 'recruited under conditions of criminal compulsion scarcely distinguishable from slave raiding and slave trading'. The Spanish were forced to turn to British-ruled Nigeria and to slightly improve conditions on the plantations.

94 **Historia geográfica de la isla de Fernando Póo.** (A geographical history of the island of Fernando Po.)
Abelardo de Unzueta y Yuste. Madrid: Instituto de Estudios Africanos, 1947. 494p. maps. bibliog.
This is the most outstanding work on the pre-World War II history, politics and religious institutions of Fernando Po. Although Unzueta y Yuste also wrote a book on Río Muni (see item no. 95), there has been no similarly thorough work done on the mainland province. Includes a preface by José M. Cordero Torres and twenty-three maps and thirty-eight illustrations.

Travels in West Africa: Congo Français, Corisco and Cameroons.
See item no. 20.

Opúsculo sobre la colonización de Fernando Póo y revista de los principales establecimientos europeos en la costa occidental de Africa. (A tract on the colonization of Fernando Po and a review of the principal European establishments on the west coast of Africa.)
See item no. 71.

Los bubis en Fernando Póo. (The Bubis of Fernando Po.)
See item no. 102.

Die Bubi auf Fernando Poo. (The Bubi of Fernando Po.)
See item no. 119.

Introduction to the Fernandian tongue.
See item no. 126.

Río Muni

95   **Guinea Continental Española.** (Continental Spanish Guinea.)
Abelardo de Unzueta y Yuste.   Madrid: Instituto de Estudios Políticos,
1944. 294p. maps. bibliog.
Although very good in parts, this Spanish-language survey of Río Muni's history is not
as good as Unzueta's work on Fernando Po. In fact a good full-length history of Río
Muni remains to be written. Illustrations are included.

**The migration of the Fang into central Gabon during the nineteenth century: a
new interpretation.**
See item no. 104.

Die Pangwe. (The Fang.)
See item no. 118.

Corisco days: the first thirty years of the West African Mission.
See item no. 155

Annobón, Corisco and the Elobeyes

96   **Annobón: l'île oubliée.** (Annobón: the forgotten island.)
Max Liniger-Goumaz.   *Mondes et Cultures* (Académie des Sciences
d'Outre-Mer, Paris), vol. XLIV, no. 4 (1984), p. 791-829.
This excellent article in French provides an overview of Annobón's history from 1471
to 1988.

97   **Islas del Golfo de Guinea.** (Islands of the Gulf of Guinea.)
Abelardo de Unzueta y Yuste.   Madrid: Instituto de Estudios Políticos,
1945. 386p. maps. bibliog.
Accompanied by maps and other illustrations, this book surveys the geography and
history of the Elobeyes, Corisco, Annobón, Príncipe and São Tomé. The preface is by
Francisco Hernández-Pacheco.

98   **Notícia de Annobón: su geografía, historia y costumbres.** (News of
Annobón: its geography, history and customs.)
Miguel Zamora Lobach.   Madrid: Papelería Madrileña, 1962. 88p.
Written by an Annobónese native, this illustrated booklet sponsored by the
Deputación Provincial de Fernando Póo discusses the geography, history and customs
of Annobón.

The Gabon and Corisco Missions.
See item no. 154.

Corisco days: the first thirty years of the West African Mission.
See item no. 155.

Population Studies

99   **Equatorial Guinea – 1920 census.**
International Population Census Publications.   New Haven,
Connecticut: Research Publications, 1973- . (microfilm series II, no. 3).

Population studies of Equatorial Guinea are rare. The first major census in the colonial era was in 1920 before Río Muni was fully explored. Reliable statistics were not available until the 1950s (and can be found in the general source below) and since independence, estimates have taken the place of censuses. Grouped under the title 'Angola' are the official statistics for Spanish Guinea's first major census in this continuing collection of microfilmed population studies.

Small is not beautiful: the story of Equatorial Guinea.
See item no. 1.

Equatorial Guinea.
See item no. 334.

Ethnic Groups

100 **Le groupe dit 'Pahouin'.** (The group called 'Pahouin'.)
Pierre Alexandre, Jacques Binet.   Paris: Presses Universitaires de
France, 1958. 152p. maps. bibliog.
The use of the term 'Pahouin' to mean Fang is unclear in origin but the mysteries of
this enigmatic group, which spreads from the Congo Republic, through Gabon and Río
Muni and into Cameroon, have fascinated many European scholars. In this classic
work in French on the Fang and related groups, Alexandre and Binet present a broad
understanding of the tribe, its language, background, folkways and beliefs. Maps and
tables are included.

101 **En el bosque Fang.** (In the Fang forest.)
I. X. de Aranzadi.   Barcelona, Spain, 1981. 250p.
This fairly recent work is perhaps the best ethnology of the Fang in Spanish.

102 **Los bubis en Fernando Póo.** (The Bubis of Fernando Po.)
Antonio Aymemi.   Madrid: Galo Saez, 1942. 198p.
This is a collection of articles on the Bubi originally published in *La Guinea española*.

103 **A dictionary of black African civilization.**
Edited by Georges Balandier, Jacques Maquet.   New York: Leon
Amiel, 1974. 350p.
A good but brief description of the Fang is offered by this general reference compiled
by two leading French Africanists.

104   **The migration of the Fang into central Gabon during the nineteenth century: a new interpretation.**
Christopher Chamberlain. *International Journal of African Historical Studies*, vol. XI, no. 3 (1978), p. 429-56.
Much scholarly speculation has been focused on the origins of the Fang tribe. Early writers mistakenly thought that they were nomadic. Others claimed that the group was displaced from lands to the north by the Fulani jihads of the 1700s. They were believed to have arrived in the forest of Río Muni around the same time that Europeans were exploring the coast (1820 to 1890). Chamberlain analyses these theories and presents a probable scenario which combines a number of these strands of thinking.

105   **Los Bayeles, una tribu pigmea en la Guinea Española.** (The Bayeles: a pygmy tribe of Spanish Guinea.)
Carlos Crespo Gil-Delgado, Count of Castillo-Fiel. *Africa* (Madrid), nos 83-84 (Nov.-Dec. 1948), p. 402-96.
One of the best of a very few brief studies on the Bayele pygmy tribes of Río Muni. Illustrations are included.

106   **Notas para un estudio antropológico y etnológico del Bubi de Fernando Póo.** (Notes for an anthropological and ethnological study of the Bubis of Fernando Po.)
Carlos Crespo Gil-Delgado, Count of Castillo-Fiel. Madrid: Instituto de Estudios Africanos, 1949. 290p.
Written by a Spanish nobleman, this anthropological and ethnological work on the Bubi is heavily influenced by official Spanish views, as is evident in its preface by José Díaz de Villegas y Bustamente. Its illustrations are worthy of mention.

107   **Africa and the West: intellectual responses to European culture.**
Edited by Philip D. Curtin. Madison, Wisconsin: University of Wisconsin Press, 1972. 259p. bibliog.
This excellent general work on European influences and African reactions to them includes as its first chapter 'Fang Representations under Acculturation' by James Fernandez (p. 3-48).

108   **La persona pamue desde le punto de vista biotipológico.** (The Fang person from a biotypological point of view.)
J. Fernández Cabezas. Madrid: Instituto de Estudios Africanos, 1951. 80p.
This illustrated monograph seeks to categorize the Fang anthropologically, but like so many other Spanish ethnological works on Africa, racism and paternalism cloud the research.

109 **Estudios guineos.** (Guinean studies.)
Carlos González Echegaray. Madrid: Instituto de Estudios Africanos,
1959-64. 2 vols.

Compiled and published by one of Spain's leading linguists between 1959 and 1964,
Volume I of this outstanding work contains linguistic studies and Volume II
ethnological studies of Fernando Po and Río Muni. The work is illustrated.

110 **Etnologia de los Bubis.** (An ethnology of the Bubis.)
Enrique Gori Molubuela. Madrid: Instituto de Estudios Africanos,
1955.

Enrique Gori Molubuela was a Bubi scholar active in religious activities and politics.
He represented Fernando Po in the Spanish parliament from 1964 to 1968. A
participant at the 1968 Constitutional Conference which set up Equatorial Guinea, he
represented the Unión Bubi and lobbied for strong ties with Spain. At independence,
he was simultaneously Fernando Po provincial counsellor and cabinet chief at the
Foreign Ministry. He was arrested on 5 March 1969 and died in Bata Prison after his
eyes were gouged out. This book is his look at his own people and as such provides a
unique viewpoint.

111 **En el país de los Pamues.** (In the land of the Fangs.)
Emilio Guinea López. Madrid: Instituto de Estudios Africanos, 1947.
156p.

Guinea López's observations and illustrations include much descriptive material on the
Fang and on the botany of Río Muni.

112 **En el país de los Bubis.** (In the land of the Bubis.)
Emilio Guinea López. Madrid: Instituto de Estudios Africanos, 1949.
287p. maps.

Guinea López's first voyage to Fernando Po is described in this well-written Spanish-
language work on both the natural and human environment of Fernando Po. Some
colour illustrations are included.

113 **The Fang.**
New Haven: Human Relations Area Files, 1960. 49 microfiches. maps.

This microfilm collection includes ethnological information on the Fang and numerous
other African groups as well as appropriate maps and illustrations.

114 **Ishulla; panorámica líbrica de las costumbres, tradiciones y arte
populares des los Bubis de Fernando Póo.** (Ishulla: a panorama of the
customs, traditions and popular arts of the Bubis of Fernando Po.)
Domingo Manfredi Cano. Madrid: Instituto de Estudios Africanos,
1950. 162p.

A Spanish-language overview of Bubi cultural and artistic traditions written at a time
when most Bubi traditions had already been abandoned for the ways of Spain and
Catholicism.

115 **Familia y matrimonio fan.** (Fang marriage and family.)
Rafael Nzé Abuy. Madrid: Ediciones Guinea, 1985.

In 1982, Rafael Nzé Abuy was made the first Archbishop of Malabo. As Bishop of Bata he had left Equatorial Guinea in 1972 in the midst of the Macías terror. In exile he worked for the relief of Equatorial Guinean refugees. Returning to Malabo after the 1979 coup, he has worked to rebuild the country's religious institutions. This book on Fang marriage and family structures incorporates some of Archbishop Nzé Abuy's beliefs that the Fang and Catholic moral systems are compatible.

116 **Eléments de base pour une approche ethnologique et historique des Fang-Beti-Boulou.** (Basic elements for an ethnological and historical approach to the Fang-Beti-Boulou.)
Jean-Pierre Ombolo. Yaoundé: University of Yaoundé, 1984. 308p. maps.

Unlike most studies of the Fang in which the viewpoint is colonial, Gabonese or Río Munian, Professor Ombolo of the University of Yaoundé looks at the Fang and the related Beti and Boulou from a Cameroonian stance. Such a viewpoint is valuable and relevant to Equatorial Guinea given the intense cross-border trade and migration of the group. Using numerous drawings and other illustrations, Ombolo is able to provide much material on the Fang and their society, language, religion, systems of authority, music, crafts, genealogy, masks, weapons, family systems and relationships with neighbouring groups.

117 **Esquema de etnologia de los Fang Ntumu de la Guinea Española.** (An ethnological outline of the Ntumu Fang of Spanish Guinea.)
Augusto Panyella-Gómez, Jorge Sabater Pi. Madrid: Instituto de Estudios Africanos, 1959. 95p. maps.

This brief illustrated description of Fang culture looks at the Ntumu, the Fang dialect group north of the Río Benito which extends into Cameroon.

118 **Die Pangwe.** (The Fang.)
Gunther Tessmann. In: *Volkerkundliche Einzelbeschreibung eines westafrikanischen Negerstammes.* Berlin: Ernest Wasmuth, 1913. 2 vols. maps. bibliog.

Complete with music, illustrations and material on expeditions in 1904-6 and the 1907-9 Lübecker Fang Expedition, Tessmann describes the Fang, their society, customs, religion and language. This study remains largely valid due to the isolation of the Fang and their resistance to outside influences.

119 **Die Bubi auf Fernando Poo.** (The Bubi of Fernando Po.)
Gunther Tessmann. In: *Volkerkundliche Einzelbeschreibung eines westafrikanischen Negerstammes.* Hagen, Germany: Folkwang Verlag, 1923. 238p. maps. bibliog.

Although this study of the Bubi equals Tessmann's work on the Fang, it is less applicable to the Bubi today, due to the almost complete disappearance of traditional Bubi culture as a result of Spanish, Nigerian, Fang and other outside influences.

Ethnic Groups

However, as a historical piece, this work, as well as Tessmann's other ethnological writings, is essential material for the modern scholar.

120   **Etnografía de Guinea: algunos grupos immigrantes de Fernando Póo.**
(Guinean ethnography: some immigrant groups of Fernando Po.)
Abelardo de Unzueta y Yuste.   *Africa* (Madrid), nos 77-78 (May-June 1948), p. 28-31.
In this short article Unzueta y Yuste examines the composition of the Fernandinos and other immigrant groups on Fernando Po.

121   **Contribución al estudio del negro Africano: Los Bujeba (Bisío) de la Guinea Española.** (A contribution to the study of the African negro: the Bujeba of Spanish Guinea.)
Antonio de Veciana Vilaldach.   Madrid: Instituto de Estudios Africanos, 1956. 166p. maps. bibliog.
Sometimes called the Bisío by the Spanish, the Bujeba are a small but historically significant Ndowe group on the coast of Río Muni. This study includes tables and graphs.

Small is not beautiful: the story of Equatorial Guinea.
See item no. 1.

Travels in West Africa: Congo Français, Corisco and Cameroons.
See item no. 20.

Eine Afrikanische Tropen-insel Fernando Poo. (A tropical African island: Fernando Po.)
See item no. 88.

The Fernandinos: labor and community in Santa Isabel de Fernando Po, 1827-1931.
See item no. 92.

Beiträge zur Kenntniss der Bubisprache auf Fernando Poo. (Contributions to the knowledge of the Bubi language of Fernando Po.)
See item no. 123.

Bwiti: an ethnography of the religious imagination in Africa.
See item no. 142.

Fetishism in West Africa: forty years' observations of native customs and superstitions.
See item no. 144.

Equatorial Guinea – Macías country: the forgotten refugees.
See item no. 174.

Minority oppression in Equatorial Guinea.
See item no. 200.

Wit and wisdom from West Africa.
See item no. 280.

La Guinée équatoriale, un pays méconnu. (Equatorial Guinea: the misunderstood land.)
See item no. 333.

Languages

122 **Gramática annobónesa.** (An Annobónese grammar.)
Natalio Barrena. Madrid: Instituto de Estudios Africanos, 1957. 95p.

The Annobónese or Ambú language is a Portuguese creole dialect with Spanish, Angolan and Bubi influences. This is one of a very few studies of this tongue spoken today by only about 1,500 people.

123 **Beiträge zur Kenntniss der Bubisprache auf Fernando Poo.**
(Contributions to the knowledge of the Bubi language of Fernando Po.)
Oskar Baumann. *Zeitschrift fur Afrikanische Sprachen* (Berlin), 1888.
p. 143-55.

This early article was among the first scholarly language studies of the Bubi not written by a missionary. Its influence on the scholars who followed was very great. See item no. 88.

124 **Diccionario español–Pamue y Pamue–español.** (A Spanish–Fang and Fang–Spanish dictionary.)
A. Bolados Carter. Santa Isabel: Vicariato Apostólico de Fernando Póo, 1900.

An early and incomplete attempt by the Roman Catholic clergy in Spanish Guinea to compile a Spanish reference on the Fang language.

125   **La influencia de las lenguas nativas en el español de la Guinea Ecuatorial.** (The influence of native languages on the Spanish of Equatorial Guinea.)
Manuel Castillo Barríl.   *Archivos del Instituto de Estudios Africanos* (Madrid), vol. II, no. 79 (1966), p. 46-71.

Written by Annobónese intellectual Manuel Castillo Barríl, a victim of the terror under Macías, this important work reviews the local contributions to the Spanish dialect which has emerged in Equatorial Guinea.

126   **Introduction to the Fernandian tongue.**
John Clarke.   Freeport, NY: Books for Libraries Press, 1971. 56p.

This reprint of an 1848 monograph by an English missionary provides a good short survey of the history of Fernando Po to 1848 and the Bubi language and its vocabulary, grammar and pronunciation. Also included are a phrase book and translations of a war song, hymn and fragments of the Gospel of Matthew.

127   **A language map of Africa and the adjacent islands.**
David Dalby.   London: International African Institute, 1977. 63p. maps.

A concise atlas of African languages which is good for locating the range of the Fang and Río Munian coastal languages.

128   **Diccionario español–kômbè.** (A Spanish–Kombe dictionary.)
Leoncio Fernández.   Madrid: Instituto de Estudios Africanos, 1951. 541p.

Kombe is the most important of the Ndowe group of coastal languages. This is the only major dictionary translating this tongue into a major European language.

129   **Dictionnaire Fang–Français et Français–Fang.** (A Fang–French and French–Fang dictionary.)
Samuel Galley.   Neuchâtel, Switzerland: Henri Messeitler, 1964. 588p.

This is the only comprehensive dictionary translating Fang into a major European language.

130   **Morfología y sintaxis de la lengua Bujeba.** (The morphology and syntax of the Bujeba language.)
Carlos González Echegaray.   Madrid: Instituto de Estudios Africanos, 1960. 191p.

The Bujeba are a part of the Ndowe group of coastal languages. Arriving in Río Muni from the east in the 12th century, they gained a reputation for ruggedness and were frequently employed in the Spanish naval infantry. This last fact gave rise to a desire to understand their language, a need which González Echegaray ably fills.

Languages

131 **The Bantu languages of western equatorial Africa.**
Malcolm Guthrie. London: International African Institute, 1953. 94p.
As part of this general survey of languages, Guthrie has included material on the Bube-Benga Group on pages 24-7 and the Yaoundé-Fang Group on pages 40-4.

132 **The Spanish of Equatorial Guinea: the dialect of Malabo and its implications for Spanish dialectology.**
John M. Lipski. Tübingen, Germany: Max Niemeyer Verlag, 1985. 120p.
This scholarly yet very readable analysis of the Spanish dialect of Malabo provides insights into the transformation of the Spanish language in Equatorial Guinea among the local people, in broadcasting and in relation to both Spain and Latin America. Fragments of conversations, documents and broadcasts are included as an appendix.

133 **Gramática Pāmue.** (A Fang grammar.)
Salvador Ndongo Esono. Madrid: Instituto de Estudios Africanos, 1956. 112p.
This is the first of a number of Fang grammars in Spanish written by Fangs.

134 **Gramática de la lengua Fan.** (A grammar of the Fang language.)
Rafael Nzé Abuy. Barcelona, Spain, 1974.
While in exile in Europe, Rafael Nzé Abuy, the then Bishop of Bata, wrote this grammar of his native language in Spanish.

135 **La lengua Fang o nkobo Fan.** (The Fang language or Nkobo Fan.)
Rafael Nzé Abuy. Barcelona, Spain: Ediciónes Guinea, 1986.
Although known primarily as a member of the Catholic hierarchy, Rafael Nzé Abuy, Archbishop of Malabo, is an accomplished linguist who speaks five languages fluently. This book provides a comprehensive look at the Fang language and its usage.

136 **Compendio de gramática Bubi.** (A summary of Bubi grammar.)
B. Pereda. Barcelona, Spain: Lucet, 1920. 116p.
This grammatical summary of Bubi builds on the earlier work of missionaries and of Baumann.

137 **Gramática de la lengua Benga.** (A grammar of the Benga language.)
G. Pérez, L. Sorinas. Madrid: Corazón de María, Ibérica, 1928.
The Benga were the first tribe of the Ndowe group of coastal languages to be encountered by European traders, explorers and missionaries. Their language was studied by Spanish scholars and by Robert H. Nassau (who translated the Bible into Benga), but eventually they more than any other Río Muni group were Europeanized. This is the best of a number of Spanish studies.

138   **Apuntes para las gramáticas Benga y Ambú.** (Annotations for Benga
      and Annobónese grammars.)
      Francisco Salvado y Cos.   Madrid: A. Pérez Dubrull, 1891.
This early collection of linguistic studies is most valuable for its final section on
Annobónese grammar by I. Vila.

139   **Dictionnaire Mpongwe–Français suivi d'éléments de grammaire.** (An
      Mpongwe–French dictionary with elements of grammar.)
      André Raponda Walker.   Brazzaville: Editiones St. Paul, 1961. 640p.
Although the Mpongwe language area is on the Atlantic coast south of Río Muni's
borders, this language has been historically important as a trading language in the
Muni estuary. This is the most important reference for this language.

Estudios guineos. (Guinean studies.)
See item no. 109.

Bwiti: an ethnography of the religious imagination in Africa.
See item no. 142.

Wit and wisdom from West Africa.
See item no. 280.

Religion

Traditional African

140 **Du Mvett: essai sur la dynastie Ekang Nna.** (Of the Mvet: essay on the
Ekang Nna dynasty.)
D. Assoumu Ndoutombe.   Paris: L'Harmattan, 1986. 184p.

The Mvet is a guitar-like musical instrument used on social and religious occasions by
the Fang. As the wandering minstrels of the Fang religion, the Mvet balladeers
chronicled the events of the group's history. Assoumu Ndoutombe relates the religion
of the Fang in a unique way in this recent French work.

141 **Drugs and mysticism: the Bwiti of the Fang.**
Jacques Binet.   *Diogènes* (Paris), vol. LXXXVI (Summer 1974),
p. 31-54.

This article highlights the use of marijuana and the hallucinogen *iboga* in Bwiti rituals
similar to Christian communion.

142 **Bwiti: an ethnography of the religious imagination in Africa.**
James W. Fernandez.   Princeton, New Jersey: Princeton University
Press, 1982. 731p. bibliog.

This excellently detailed work on the religious beliefs and practices of the Fang is the
result of years of experience and painstaking research on the part of Fernandez.
Research was undertaken mainly in Gabon, but much information is included on Río
Muni. Included are chapters on Fang–European contacts, beliefs regarding space, time
and the past, resource distribution, sexual relations, authority, initiation rites, the
occult, ritual, morality, religious architecture, liturgy, music, dreams, visions, morality,
linguistics and healing. Three useful appendices include a glossary of terms, texts of
Bwiti sermons and information on Mbiri societies. The numerous illustrations and
photographs throughout the book are the work of Fernandez and his wife, Renate.

143   **La naissance à l'envers: essai sur le rituel du Bwiti Fang au Gabon.**
(Birth on the wrong side: an essay on the Bwiti Fang ritual of Gabon.)
André Mary.   Paris: L'Harmattan, 1983. 384p. bibliog. discog. filmog.
Concentrating on the artistic, mystical and literary side of Fang traditional religion, Mary's study of Gabonese Bwiti ritual is equally applicable to southern Río Muni.

144   **Fetishism in West Africa: forty years' observations of native customs and superstitions.**
Robert H. Nassau.   New York: Negro Universities Press, 1969. 389p. map.
From 1861 to 1898, Robert Hamill Nassau was an American Presbyterian missionary in what was to become Río Muni and Gabon. The first ten years of his ministry were spent on Corisco Island where he evangelized the Benga. His contributions to linguistics, tropical medicine, ethnology and religious studies have been enormous, particularly because he was an excellent observer who was relatively free of the ethnocentric views of his age. This is his principal work on local religious beliefs. This edition, which includes twelve illustrations, is a reprint of his original by Scribners for the Young People's Missionary Movement in 1904.

145   **La secta del Bwiti en la Guinea Española.** (The Bwiti sect in Spanish Guinea.)
Antonio de Veciana Vilaldach.   Madrid: Instituto de Estudios Africanos, 1958. 63p. bibliog.
This short work on the Bwiti religion among the Río Muni Fang is good but marked by some colonial prejudices. Illustrations are included.

Small is not beautiful: the story of Equatorial Guinea.
See item no. 1.

Equatorial Guinea: an African tragedy.
See item no. 63.

Equatorial Guinea – Macías country: the forgotten refugees.
See item no. 174.

The affirmation of things past: Alar Ayong and Bwiti as movements of protest in central and northern Gabon.
See item no. 179.

Roman Catholicism

146 **Segunda memoria de las misiones de Fernando Póo y sus dependencias.**
(Memoirs of the missions in Fernando Po and its dependencies.)
Armengol Coll. Madrid: Imprenta Iberia de E. Maestre, 1911. 110p.
In 1904 Spanish priest Father Armengol Coll became the first Bishop of the Apostolic
Prefecture of Fernando Po. His memoirs describe the efforts of missionaries on the
island.

147 **Misiones y misioneros en la Guinea Española.** (Missions and
missionaries in Spanish Guinea.)
Cristobal Fernández. Madrid: Editorial Co. SA, 1962. 817p.
A well-documented history of the Roman Catholic missionary activity in Spanish
Guinea from 1883 to 1912.

148 **La Iglesia en la Guinea Ecuatorial.** (The Church in Equatorial Guinea.)
Tomas L. Pujadas. Madrid: Impresa de Paz, 1968. new edition, 1985.
528p.
Pujadas' impressive work is the only history of the Catholic Church in Equatorial
Guinea which is close to comprehensive.

149 **La Iglesia reducida al silencio.** (The Church reduced to silence.)
A. Salas. *Mundo Negro* (Madrid), vol. XIX, no. 204 (Oct. 1978),
p. 38-43.
This article examines the silence of the Roman Catholic Church during the human
rights violations of the Macías era.

Small is not beautiful: the story of Equatorial Guinea.
See item no. 1.

Adventures and observations on the west coast of Africa and its islands.
See item no. 22.

Equatorial Guinea: an African tragedy.
See item no. 63.

Persécutions religieuses en Guinée Equatoriale. (Religious persecution in
Equatorial Guinea.)
See item no. 206.

**L'évolution des structures productives et sociales de l'économie de la Guinée
Equatoriale 1858-1968.** (The evolution of the productive and social structures
of the economy of Equatorial Guinea 1858-1968.)
See item no. 230.

Protestantism

150 **One hundred years: a history of the foreign missionary work of the Presbyterian Church in the USA.**
Arthur J. Brown. New York: Revell, 1936. 240p.
As the first and most successful Protestant mission in Río Muni, the American Presbyterian Church established a strong presence in the Muni estuary. Pages 196 to 250 of this general look at Presbyterian missionary work deal with missions in Africa, including those started by James Love Mackey and Robert Hamill Nassau on Corisco.

151 **The beginnings of Christian evangelism and African responses: American Presbyterians in Equatorial Guinea and Gabon.**
Penelope Campbell. *Papers presented at the 19th Annual Meeting of the African Studies Association* (Boston), 3-6 Nov. 1976. 27p. (Paper no. 15).
Campbell's paper provides an excellent overview of the environment faced by early Presbyterian missionaries in equatorial Africa.

152 **American Protestant evangelism and African responses: the American Presbyterians in Gabon and Equatorial Guinea.**
Penelope Campbell. *Papers presented at the December 1977 American Historical Association meeting* (Dallas), 1977. 22p.
This paper continues but repeats much of item no. 151.

153 **Cameroons and Fernando Po.**
J. J. Fuller. London: Baptist Missionary Society, 1887. 22p. (Unpublished manuscript).
The son of a freed slave, Jackson Fuller, and a carpenter-turned-missionary, Alfred Saker, set up a Baptist mission school on Fernando Po. The Baptists established themselves well throughout the 1840s, but the reaffirmation of Spanish colonial rule in the 1850s caused them to be expelled to Cameroon where they founded the Victoria Mission from which the city of Victoria was built. Fuller's collection of writings is an important document in the history of missions in the region.

154 **The Gabon and Corisco Missions.**
Robert H. Nassau. New York: Presbyterian Board of Foreign Missions, 1873.
In this tract, Nassau discusses the then newly established Presbyterian missions in equatorial Africa. See also item no. 144.

155 **Corisco days: the first thirty years of the West African Mission.**
Robert H. Nassau. Philadelphia, Pennsylvania: Allen, Lane and Scott, 1910.
This work is a large part of Nassau's African memoirs and includes numerous observations of religion, life and history on Corisco and along the neighbouring coast. See also item no. 144.

156 **Africa and the United Presbyterians.**
W. T. Thomas, E. B. Faiman. New York: United Presbyterian
Church in America, 1959.

An overview of Presbyterian church activity in Africa, centred on Gabon and Río
Muni.

157 **Worldwide thrust.**
Ft. Washington, Pennsylvania: WEC International, Jan.-Feb. 1987.
10p.

A Protestant missionary tract containing 'My Name Appeared on the Death List' by
Antonio Ntutumo Ncogo and 'Please do not abandon us' by Elliott Tepper, both of
which describe religious persecution under Macías and the renewal of their church
after the 1979 coup.

Adventures and observations on the west coast of Africa and its islands.
See item no. 22.

Equatorial Guinea: an African tragedy.
See item no. 63.

Persécutions religieuses en Guinée Equatoriale. (Religious persecution in
Equatorial Guinea.)
See item no. 206.

**Robert Hamill Nassau 1835-1921: Presbyterian pioneer missionary to
equatorial west Africa.**
See item no. 327.

Social Conditions

158 **The sociology of black Africa.**
Georges Balandier.   London: André Deutsch, 1970. 540p.
This general work on the sociology of the African continent is particularly strong in accessing the impact of colonialization and Western influence on African societies, especially among the Fang who are one of Balandier's favourite subjects of study.

159 **Living conditions in Equatorial Guinea.**
United Nations.   New York: United Nations Development Programme, 11 August 1975. (Document UNDP/ADM/Post/EQG/Rev. 3).
Intended as a guide for United Nations personnel, this document describes the desperate state into which Equatorial Guinea had fallen after six years of independence, misrule, corruption and human rights abuses. Unsanitary conditions, disease, lack of transport and electricity and shortages of food, medicines, light bulbs, batteries, fuel and other essential products are all documented in some detail. Suggestions are made for personnel going to the country.

Small is not beautiful: the story of Equatorial Guinea.
See item no. 1.

Equatorial Guinea post report.
See item no. 4.

Report of the International Commission of Inquiry into the existence of slavery and forced labor in the Republic of Liberia.
See item no. 93.

Equatorial Guinea – Macías country: the forgotten refugees.
See item no. 174.

Social Conditions

Equatorial Guinea: colonialism, state terror and the search for stability.
See item no. 175.

Equatorial Guinea: the forgotten dictatorship.
See item no. 199.

Health

160 **Observations on the fevers of the west coast of Africa.**
Henry A. Ford.   New York: Edward Jenkins, 1856.
This early work on diseases in the humid regions of tropical Africa's Atlantic coast
provides not only information on the 'fevers' for scholars and travellers of the day, but
also material on early attitudes regarding health in the tropics.

161 **Organización del servicio sanitario en las provincias de Fernando Póo y
Río Muni.** (The organization of health services in the provinces of
Fernando Po and Río Muni.)
J. Gascón Briega.   *Africa* (Madrid), nos 260-261 (Aug.-Sept. 1963),
p. 413.
For much of its history Equatorial Guinea has had extremely poor medical and
sanitation services. This article describes the vastly improved health and sanitation
services which were established in Spanish Guinea during the period of 'provincialization' in the early 1960s.

162 **Aspectos de la lucha sanitaria en Guinea.** (Aspects of the struggle for
public health in Guinea.)
C. López-Motra.   *Archivos del Instituto de Estudios Africanos*
(Madrid), no. 9 (Aug. 1949), p. 7-16.
López-Motra provides a view of health and sanitation which is extremely generous to
the Spanish colonial administration.

163 **El pasado y presente de la sanidad en Guinea como base para la actuación en el futuro.** (The past and present of public health in Guinea as a basis for future action.)
R. Majo Framis. Madrid: Instituto de Estudios Africanos, 1968. 14p.
By the time of independence the colonial administration in Spanish Guinea had improved health care to the extent that the ratio of hospital beds per capita was higher in the colony than in Spain itself. This short study outlining the health situation is no. 17 in the African Monograph Series of the Instituto de Estudios Africanos.

164 **Estudio epidemiológico y clínico de la endemia de la lepra en la Guinea española.** (An epidemiological and clinical study of leprosy in Spanish Guinea.)
V. Martínez Domínguez. Madrid: Instituto de Estudios Africanos, 1954. 113p.
Spanish Guinea had 4,000 to 5,000 lepers in the 1940s. After great efforts to eradicate the disease, leprosy-related deaths declined to eight in 1962 and freedom from the disease was within grasp by the time of independence. As a result of the neglect of health care by the Macías régime, leprosy regained a foothold in the 1970s. This study of the disease, which includes seven tables, fourteen drawings and 105 photographs, was conducted at a time when Spanish colonial health services were treating around 3,000 patients in sanitoriums.

165 **Progresos sanitarias en la Guinea Española.** (Progress in public health in Spanish Guinea.)
Valentin Matilla y Gómez. *Archivos del Instituto de Estudios Africanos* (Madrid), no. 55 (1960), p. 7-28.
This article on health services in Spanish Guinea is one of the best in describing the accomplishments and plans of the colonial authorities.

166 **Hemoglobina anormal en Guinea Ecuatorial.** (Abnormal haemoglobin in Equatorial Guinea.)
R. E. Modica, J. R. Flores. Santa Isabel: World Health Organization, August 1969. 28p.
Abnormal haemoglobin, a condition common in Río Muni and Gabon is described in this specialized paper written for the guidance of WHO personnel in the country.

Small is not beautiful: the story of Equatorial Guinea.
See item no. 1.

Equatorial Guinea – Macías country: the forgotten refugees.
See item no. 174.

Equatorial Guinea: colonialism, state terror and the search for stability.
See item no. 175.

Migration, Exiles and Refugees

167 **Equatorial Guinea: fascism and slavery.**
The Guardian (New York), 15 Dec. 1976, p. 13-17.
This report in an American radical weekly looks at the overall situation in Equatorial Guinea under Macías, but concentrates on the activities of exiles, particularly those of the Geneva-based Alianza Nacional de Restauración Democratica (the National Alliance for the Restoration of Democracy).

168 **La voz del pueblo.** (The voice of the people.)
Information Office of the Alianza Nacional de Restauración Democratica.   Geneva: ANRD, 1976-87. irregular.
Although representing an extremely anti-Nguemist viewpoint, this occasional publication of the leading Equatorial Guinean exile organization is good not only on exile politics and other refugee activities but also on the internal situation and foreign relations of Equatorial Guinea.

169 **La voz del pueblo: suplemento.** (The voice of the people: supplement.)
Information Office of ANRD.   Geneva: ANRD, April 1977.
ANRD is the leading Equatorial Guinean exile movement and *La Voz del Pueblo* is its news periodical. As one would expect, its views are not objective. However, this booklet which is one of their occasional publications contains fifty-one photocopies of articles on Equatorial Guinea from the world press, including twenty-five in French, thirteen in Spanish and thirteen in English. Photographs and other illustrations are included, though sometimes as dark reproductions.

170 **La voz del pueblo: suplemento no. 3.** (The voice of the people: supplement 3.)
Information Office of ANRD. Geneva: ANRD, July 1983. 130p.

A continuation of item no. 169, containing 136 photocopies of articles on Equatorial Guinea from the world press, including sixty-one in Spanish, fifty-two in French and thirteen in English.

171 **Situación social y promoción de los guineanos en Madrid.** (The social situation and promotion of Guineans in Madrid.)
Madrid: Asociación de Amigos de Guinea Ecuatorial (ASODAGE), 1978. 90p.

ASODAGE is a non-political charity dedicated to aiding Equatorial Guinean refugees in Spain. This report provides a profile of the refugee community and describes the situation of refugees living in Spain in terms of employment, housing, living conditions and social and religious activities.

172 **La décolonisation de la Guinée Equatoriale et le problème des réfugies.** (The decolonization of Equatorial Guinea and the refugee problem.)
C. M. Eya Nchama. *Genève-Afrique* (Geneva), vol. XX, no. 1 (1982), p. 73-128.

This excellent journal article by the main Equatorial Guinean exile leader provides a wealth of information on the history of refugees and exiles both to and from Equatorial Guinea. Included are descriptions of the freed slaves and First World War German troops as refugees on Fernando Po and the political and economic exiles of the colonial and Macías eras. Numerous other historical facts included in this work are of more general interest.

173 **Rencontre avec le leader de l'opposition, les exilés équato-guinéens se méfient du successeur de l'ex-dictateur.** (Encounter with the opposition leader, the Equatorial Guinean exiles are suspicious of the ex-dictator's successor.)
Etienne Ugueux. *Le Soir* (Brussels), 26-27 Aug. 1979.

An extensive interview with ANRD leader Eya Nchama by the Belgian newspaper, *Le Soir*, underlines the exiles' doubts that conditions will improve under Teodoro Obiang Nguema.

Equatorial Guinea: an African tragedy.
See item no. 63.

Los confinados a Fernando Póo e impresiones de un viaje a Guinea. (The exiles to Fernando Po and impressions of a journey to Guinea.)
See item no. 87.

The Fernandinos: labor and community in Santa Isabel de Fernando Po, 1827-1931.
See item no. 92.

Report of the International Commission of Inquiry into the existence of slavery and forced labor in the Republic of Liberia.
See item no. 93.

The migration of the Fang into central Gabon during the nineteenth century: a new interpretation.
See item no. 104.

Equatorial Guinea – Macías country: the forgotten refugees.
See item no. 174.

Equatorial Guinea: the forgotten dictatorship.
See item no. 199.

Politics

General

174 **Equatorial Guinea – Macías country: the forgotten refugees.**
Robert af Klinteberg. Geneva: International University Exchange
Fund, 1978. 87p. maps.

A somewhat disorganized report by a Swedish anthropologist and human rights
advocate who entered Equatorial Guinea as a businessman in 1978. Many valuable
insights and interviews are provided, as well as a biography of Francisco Macías
Nguema. Klinteberg is particularly strong in presenting material, much of it unique, on
living conditions, forced labour, dictatorial rule, torture and the Equatorial Guinean
refugee situations in Gabon, Cameroon, Nigeria, Spain and elsewhere. Some
interviews and quotes are exceptional. Diagrams, maps and tables are included.

175 **Equatorial Guinea: colonialism, state terror and the search for stability.**
Ibrahim K. Sundiata. Boulder, Colorado: Westview, 1990. 179p.
bibliog.

Although this concise, but excellent, book is centred on the political history of
Equatorial Guinea, many other aspects of the country are covered and accompanied by
the most recent statistics available. Sections include details of the country's geography,
cultures, economy, labour issues, religion, education, language, the status of women
and health. Black-and-white photographs are scattered throughout the text.

Small is not beautiful: the story of Equatorial Guinea.
See item no. 1.

Equatorial Guinea: an African tragedy.
See item no. 63.

Historia y tragedia de Guinea Ecuatorial. (The history and tragedy of Equatorial Guinea.)
See item no. 64.

Congo, Gabon, Equatorial Guinea: country report, analyses of economic and political trends.
See item no. 231.

Gabon, Equatorial Guinea: country profile, annual survey of political and economic background.
See item no. 232.

Quarterly review of Gabon, Congo, Cameroon, the Central African Republic, Chad and Equatorial Guinea.
See item no. 233.

La Guinée équatoriale, un pays méconnu. (Equatorial Guinea: the misunderstood land.)
See item no. 333.

Equatorial Guinea.
See item no. 334.

Colonial administration

176 **El régimen juridico-financiero colonial.** (The colonial juridical-financial régime.)
J. Gómez Duran. Madrid: Instituto de Estudios Africanos, 1946. 350p.
Although clearly and obviously prejudiced in favour of Spain's imperial role in Africa, Gómez Duran's work provides a good and comprehensive look at the colonial system prior to any reforms which resulted from anti-colonial pressures.

177 **El Africanismo español.** (Spanish Africanism.)
L. Saez de Govantes. Madrid: Instituto de Estudios Africanos, 1971.
In an attempt to encourage newly independent Equatorial Guinea to maintain close ties with her former colonial master, Luis Saez de Govantes describes the historic connections between Spain and her former colony.

178 **Política indígena en Guinea.** (Native politics in Guinea.)
A. Yglesias de la Riva. Madrid: Instituto de Estudios Africanos, 1947. 366p. bibliog.
A Spanish view of colonial rule and administration on Fernando Po and in Río Muni prior to the first rumblings of discontent among teachers which led to the long campaign for independence.

Plazas y provincias africanas españolas. (Spanish African towns and provinces.)
See item no. 26.

Equatorial Guinea: an African tragedy.
See item no. 63.

Reivindicaciones de España. (Vindications of Spain.)
See item no. 65.

Spanish Guinea: enclave empire.
See item no. 67.

De colonización y económia en la Guinea española. (Concerning colonization and economics in Spanish Guinea.)
See item no. 77.

Equatorial Guinea: colonialism, state terror and the search for stability.
See item no. 175.

L'évolution des structures productives et sociales de l'économie de la Guinée Equatoriale 1858-1968. (The evolution of the productive and social structures of the economy of Equatorial Guinea 1858-1968.)
See item no. 230.

Political organizations

179 **The affirmation of things past: Alar Ayong and Bwiti as movements of protest in central and northern Gabon.**
James Fernandez. In: *Protest and Power in Black Africa*, edited by Robert Rotberg, Ali Mazrui. New York: Oxford University Press, 1970, p. 427-57.
Founded in the 1940s, the Alar Ayong was a Fang messianic movement and secret society connected with the Bwiti cult. It sheltered those in trouble with the authorities and acted as a social organization for Fang youth. Spreading from Cameroon to Río Muni and Gabon, it became politicized and chauvinistic. The French were able to bring Alar Ayong members into the mainstream of Gabonese political life and tone down the more negative features of the movement. However, the Spanish did little to alter their system and neither the affirmation of the past written of by Fernandez nor political recognition in the near future were accorded to the Río Muni Fang.

180 **Political movements in Spanish Guinea.**
René Pélissier. *Africa Report*, vol. 9 (May 1964), p. 3-7.
With the increasing international pressure on Spain for decolonization, Pélissier looks at the Equatorial Guinean political movements which had been established to press for independence. Note that this article was written before either Bubi separatism or Macías' influence was an issue.

Equatorial Guinea: an African tragedy.
See item no. 63.

Political handbook of the world.
See item no. 191.

Post-colonial dictatorships

181 Psychoses of power: African personal dictatorships.
Samuel Decalo.   Boulder, Colorado: Westview, 1989. 222p.

As a political psychologist, Decalo analyses the three most brutal African dictators of modern times: Francisco Macías Nguema of Equatorial Guinea, Idi Amin of Uganda and Jean-Bedel Bokassa of the Central African Republic. Chapter two on Equatorial Guinea considers that country's socio-economic background, the politics of the independence era, a biography of Macías, Macías' reign of terror and its effects, Macías' overthrow and the first years of the rule of Teodoro Obiang Nguema. In Chapters one and five, Decalo provides the general theoretical basis and conclusions of his work and in doing so comments on the conditions which have led to abusive rule in the three countries of his study.

182 Equatorial Guinea: after the coup.
Karen Gellen.   *The Guardian* (New York), 24 Oct. 1979, p. 22.

In examining the August 1979 coup, this radical paper expresses concern that the new leader, Macías' nephew Obiang, would hardly change the country's brutal and corrupt post-independence record.

183 Personal rule in black Africa
Robert H. Jackson, Carl G. Rosberg.   Berkeley, California: University of California Press, 1982. 316p.

Jackson and Rosberg combine biography, psychology and political theory to develop a system of categorizing African leaders into four major archetypes: prince, autocrat, prophet and tyrant. Leading their list of tyrants and the subject of a seven-page biography is Francisco Macías Nguema, Equatorial Guinea's first president.

184 Guinée Equatoriale de la dictature des colons à la dictature des colonels.
(Equatorial Guinea from the dictatorship of colonialists to the dictatorship of the colonels.)
Max Liniger-Goumaz.   Geneva: Editions du Temps, 1982. 230p.

This book, complete with a section of eight black-and-white photographs in the centre, is Liniger-Goumaz's first major work following the 1979 coup. Following a 45-page general introduction on the country, the rules of Macías and Obiang are described and compared. Finished after Pope John Paul II's February 1982 visit to Equatorial Guinea, the author warns that not all is well in the country.

Politics. Post-colonial dictatorships

185   **De la Guinée Equatoriale Nguemiste: éléments pour le dossier de l'Afro-Fascism.** (Of Nguemist Equatorial Guinea: elements for the dossier on Afro-Fascism.)
Max Liniger-Goumaz.   Geneva: Editions du Temps, 1983. 270p.
Clearly dismayed by the increasing international recognition of the Obiang régime, Liniger-Goumaz continues to document events in Equatorial Guinea and point out the authoritarianism of the régime. A section of black-and-white photographs is included.

186   **Guinea Ecuatorial: polémica y realidad.** (Equatorial Guinea: polemics and reality.)
Constantino Ochaga Mve Bengobesama.   Madrid: Ediciones Guinea, 1985.
A cousin of Obiang, Ochaga Mve Bengobesama has had high-ranking posts in the Ministry of Education since 1979 and was appointed Minister of Transport, Communications and Tourism in 1982. This book demonstrates his clear commitment to Obiang's dictatorship and is an attempt to counter accusations of continued human rights violations, corruption and mismanagement which have been levelled against the régime by human rights organizations, exiles, international bodies and the press.

187   **Autopsy of a miracle.**
René Pélissier.   *Africa Report* (May-June 1980), p. 10-14.
This short article, accompanied by a number of interesting photographs, provides an excellent look at Macías' final days in power, the August 1979 coup and its aftermath. It is important both as a fragment of political history and as an account of the conclusion of Macías' life.

188   **Equatorial Guinea: the structure of terror in a small state.**
Ibrahim K. Sundiata.   In: *African Islands and Enclaves*, edited by R. Cohen. Beverley Hills, California: Sage, 1983, p. 81-100.
With the benefit of both hindsight and careful research, Sundiata looks at the magnitude of the terror which seized Equatorial Guinea under Macías in relation to the country's small size and evaluates the conditions which enabled such a dictatorship to survive so long.

189   **The roots of African despotism: the question of political culture.**
Ibrahim K. Sundiata.   *African Studies Review*, vol. XXXI, no. 1 (April 1988), p. 9-31.
In this article, Sundiata examines the origins of authoritarian rule in Africa, especially colonialism and lack of political education and experience. He uses Equatorial Guinea as his main example.

Tropical gangsters.
See item no. 23.

Aekvatorialguinea. (Equatorial Guinea.)
See item no. 24.

Equatorial Guinea: an African tragedy.
See item no. 63.

Guinea: materia reservada. (Guinea: reserved material.)
See item no. 81.

Guinea: Macías, la ley del silencio. (Guinea: Macías, the rule of silence.)
See item no. 82.

Prelude to scandal.
See item no. 86.

Equatorial Guinea – Macías country: the forgotten refugees.
See item no. 174.

Equatorial Guinea: colonialism, state terror and the search for stability.
See item no. 175.

La Guinée Equatoriale et la démocratisation: l'astucieux recours à un 'constitutionnalisme rédhibitoire' de 1982. (Equatorial Guinea and democratization: the crafty recourse to reactionary constitutionalism in 1982.)
See item no. 194.

Military trials and the use of the death penalty in Equatorial Guinea.
See item no. 198.

Equatorial Guinea: the forgotten dictatorship.
See item no. 199.

Equatorial Guinea: machinations in founding a national bank.
See item no. 244.

Toda la verdad: mi intervención en Guinea. (All the truth: my intervention in Guinea.)
See item no. 321.

Interview with Macías.
See item no. 324.

Constitutions and legal system

190 **The trial of Macías in Equatorial Guinea – the story of a dictatorship.**
A. Artucio.   Paris: International Commission of Jurists, 1979. 75p.
This report by an expert of the International Commission of Jurists examines the procedures and conduct of the 1979 trial of Francisco Macías Nguema which resulted in his death sentence and in the suppression of evidence which would implicate members of the new régime in the human rights violations of the 1969-79 period.

Politics. Constitutions and legal system

191 **Political handbook of the world.**
Edited by A. J. Banks.   New York: McGraw-Hill. annual.
Since 1976 the Center for Comparative Political Research at the State University of New York at Binghamton has produced this annual reference which reports on political structures (governments, inter-governmental organizations, political parties, etc.) and regional issues around the world. The constitution of Equatorial Guinea and its early revisions by Macías is surveyed in the 1976 issue on pages 94-6. Issues since that time have provided additional details of the Equatorial Guinean political system.

192 **New constitution in Equatorial Guinea.**
International Commission of Jurists.   *ICJ Review* (Geneva), no. 29 (Dec. 1982), p. 3-6.
This article points out the many authoritarian or potentially authoritarian attributes of the 1982 Equatorial Guinean Constitution which could threaten the full restoration of human rights in the country.

193 **The basic law of Equatorial Guinea.**
Government of Equatorial Guinea.   Malabo: National Commission for the Constitution, 3 Aug. 1982. 62p.
The official bulletin of state containing the text of the Equatorial Guinean Constitution of 1982.

194 **La Guinée Equatoriale et la démocratisation: l'astucieux recours à un 'constitutionnalisme rédhibitoire' de 1982.** (Equatorial Guinea and democratization: the crafty recourse to reactionary constitutionalism in 1982.)
Joseph Owona.   *Le Mois en Afrique* (Paris), no. 207-8 (April-May 1983), p. 59-68.
This article by a Cameroonian law professor provides an article-by-article critique of the Equatorial Guinean Constitution of 1982. Owona is in agreement with the many other scholars and human rights activists who see this constitution as a shield for continued dictatorial rule.

195 **Equatorial Guinea**
A. A. Rodriguez.   In: *Constitutions of the Countries of the World.*
New York: Blauenstein & Flanz, 1974. 3 vols.
The Equatorial Guinea section of this reference work provides the text of the Equatorial Guinean constitution as it stood in 1973.

196 **A new constitution in Equatorial Guinea: written declaration presented by the International Commission of Jurists**
Geneva: UN Commission on Human Rights, 31 Jan. 1983. 4p. (UN Document E/CN.4/1983/NGO/4).
This UN document encorporates the contents of item no. 192 as a critical analysis of the 1982 Equatorial Guinean Constitution.

Human Rights

197 Amnesty International reports
London: Amnesty International. annual.
Amnesty International provides in its annual reports a review of human rights violations worldwide. Equatorial Guinea has been covered by articles in issues throughout the 1970s and 1980s. Appendices related to the international protection of human rights are useful references.

198 Military trials and the use of the death penalty in Equatorial Guinea.
London: Amnesty International, 1987. 15p.
Throughout the 1980s a number of military trials and executions were conducted in Equatorial Guinea. Concerned with these events, Amnesty International released this brief report which concentrates on the Obiang régime's use of these expedients.

199 Equatorial Guinea: the forgotten dictatorship.
Suzanne Cronje.   London: British Anti-Slavery Society for the Protection of Human Rights, 1976. 43p.
Though a short report, this work was influential in publicizing the human rights violations taking place in Equatorial Guinea under Macías, 1968-79. It provides a reasonable amount of background on the case and deals in some depth with questions of forced labour, fundamental freedoms, torture, political murder, refugee problems and the inactivity of foreign countries and international organizations with regard to Equatorial Guinea's internal problems.

200 Minority oppression in Equatorial Guinea.
Randall Fegley. In: *World Minorities*, vol. II, edited by Georgina Ashworth. London: Minority Rights Group, 1978, p. 80-4.
This chapter (Ch. 19) of a general work on minorities around the world, examines both the general human rights issues and specific minority problems of Equatorial Guinea.

201 **The UN Human Rights Commission: the Equatorial Guinea case.**
Randall Fegley. *Human Rights Quarterly* (Johns Hopkins
University Press, Baltimore, Maryland), no. 1 (Feb. 1981), p. 34-47.

This journal article reviews the case of Equatorial Guinea as presented to the UN Commission of Human Rights in Geneva. Contents include material on the human rights violations of the Macías régime, international responses to the case, the UN Commission on Human Rights and its procedures and problems, the international protection of human rights, advisory services for restoring human rights and an evaluation of the Commission's role.

202 **Equatorial Guinea.**
Niall MacDermot. *Bulletin of the International Commission of Jurists*
(Geneva), no. 13 (Dec. 1974), p. 10-13.

An early commentator on the human rights situation in Equatorial Guinea, MacDermot went on to sit in the UN Commission on Human Rights as the delegate from the International Commission of Jurists. As such his observations are important. This article concentrates on Macías' elimination of political opponents.

203 **Mission concernant la Guinée Equatoriale.** (A mission relating to
Equatorial Guinea.)
Thierry Mignon. Paris: International Federation for the Rights of
Man, August 1974.

As counsel at the Court of Appeal in Paris, Mignon was dispatched by the International Federation for the Rights of Man to investigation human rights violations in Equatorial Guinea. His team was refused entry and instead conducted extensive surveys in refugee areas in Gabon. His widely circulated report condemns the Macías régime for its abuses.

204 **Guinea: de colonia a dictatura.** (Guinea: from colony to dictatorship.)
L. Mitogo. Madrid: Edicusa, 1977. 54p.

An Equatorial Guinean exile examines the evidence of human rights violations and accuses the Macías régime of mass murder.

205 **Terror grips Equatorial Guinea.**
One World (Geneva), 1 Nov. 1974, p. 7-9.

This article in the monthly magazine of the World Council of Churches describes the human rights violations, economic stagnation and political manoeuvring of the Macías régime, concentrating especially on religious persecution.

206 **Persécutions religieuses en Guinée Equatoriale.** (Religious persecution
in Equatorial Guinea.)
Parole et Société, vol. LXXXVII, no. 3 (1979), p. 184-9

This French article describes the oppression which was dealt out to religious institutions and groups under Macías.

207   **The U.N. Commission on Human Rights.**
       Howard Tolley.   Boulder, Colorado: Westview, 1987. 300p.
As an important case for the UN Human Rights Commission, Equatorial Guinea is
cited frequently and often in some detail in Tolley's technical analysis of the workings,
politics and problems of the Geneva-based Commission. But as this book is on the
Commission rather than on Equatorial Guinea, to pull out of it a full description of any
single case requires a good deal of work.

208   **Assistance to Equatorial Guinea: report of the secretary general.**
       New York: United Nations, 19 Aug. 1985. 26p.
This document is a summary of the assistance provided to Equatorial Guinea by UN
agencies seeking to revitalize the economy and restore full human rights to the
country.

209   **Economic and Social Council official records.**
       New York: United Nations. annual.
Following the close of UNCHR sessions each spring, the United Nations produces a
supplement to its Economic and Social Council's official records which reports on that
year's session of the Commission on Human Rights. Prior to 1988 this supplement was
listed as no. 5. For years 1988 to the present, sessional reports appear as Supplement
no. 2. These publicly available reports document all UNCHR business and have had
large amounts of material on Equatorial Guinea every year since 1978.

210   **The provision of expert assistance in the field of human rights:**
       Equatorial Guinea.
       Geneva: UN Commission on Human Rights, 16 Jan. 1985. 52p.
       (Document E/CN.4/1985/9).
This summary of the legal and other advisory services provided by the UN to
Equatorial Guinea also expresses concern over the lack of progress towards any true
democratization in the country.

211   **A study of the human rights situation in Equatorial Guinea.**
       Fernando Volio Jimenez.   Geneva: UN Commission on Human
       Rights, 12 Feb. 1980. 90p. maps. (Document E/CN.4/1371).
Fernando Volio Jimenez, a Costa Rican law professor, was designated Special
Rapporteur of the UNCHR for the case of Equatorial Guinea. This report is an
account of his first journey to the country in which he concluded that much freedom
had been restored but the situation was far from satisfactory. His mission was
obstructed in a number of ways and a road accident, in which Volio was injured,
reduced its abilities considerably. Many of the rapporteur's queries to officials went
unanswered and the régime showed little interest in the mission and little desire to
assist it. Volio Jimenez persevered and was able to present this excellent report to the
Commission at its 1980 session. Unlike most UN documents, this account is not only
readable but quotable and its descriptions provide many details which fill in the picture
of what life in Equatorial Guinea was like immediately after Macías.

212 **The human rights situation in Equatorial Guinea.**
Fernando Volio Jimenez. Geneva: UN Commission on Human
Rights, 19 Dec. 1980. 112p. maps. (Document E/CN.4/1439).
The record of Volio Jimenez' second and more successful tour of Equatorial Guinea
expresses continued doubts in the Obiang régime's commitment to human rights. The
rapporteur would make a number of other visits in the capacity of UN expert adviser.
The results of these missions are described in the Economic and Social Council's
official records (see item no. 209).

Equatorial Guinea: an African tragedy.
See item no. 63.

Historia y tragedia de Guinea Ecuatorial. (The history and tragedy of
Equatorial Guinea.)
See item no. 64.

Guinea: materia reservada. (Guinea: reserved material.)
See item no. 81.

Guinea: Macías, la ley del silencio. (Guinea: Macías, the rule of silence.)
See item no. 82.

Worldwide thrust.
See item no. 157.

Equatorial Guinea – Macías country: the forgotten refugees.
See item no. 174.

Equatorial Guinea: colonialism, state terror and the search for stability.
See item no. 175.

Autopsy of a miracle.
See item no. 187.

**La Guinée Equatoriale et la démocratisation: l'astucieux recours à un
'constitutionnalisme rédhibitoire' de 1982.** (Equatorial Guinea and democratization: the crafty recourse to reactionary constitutionalism in 1982.)
See item no. 194.

**Special economic assistance and disaster relief aid: assistance to Equatorial
Guinea.**
See item no. 242.

Interview with Macías.
See item no. 324.

Foreign Relations

Colonial

213   Nigeria and Fernando Poo, 1958-1966: the politics of irredentism.
B. Akinyemi.   *African Affairs*, vol. LXIX, no. 276 (July 1970),
p. 236-49.

A significant segment of Nigeria's population considers Fernando Po to be a natural
part of their country. Linked by historical, cultural, economic and labour ties,
Fernando Po and Nigeria are frequently seen to have more in common than the island
and Río Muni. Akinyemi examines Nigerian–Spanish Guinean relations in the period
just prior to the Nigerian Civil War and Equatorial Guinean independence.

214   African boundaries: a legal and diplomatic encyclopedia.
Ian Brownlie.   London: Hurst, 1979. 1355p.

This huge work, which contains numerous treaty texts, is by far the most important
reference work on national borders in Africa. Of interest to those studying Equatorial
Guinea are the sections on Equatorial Guinea, Gabon and Cameroon.

215   La délimitation des frontières du Gabon (1885-1911). (The delimitation
of the frontiers of Gabon, 1885-1911.)
A. Mangomo-Nzambi.   *Cahiers d'Etudes africaines* (Paris), vol. IX,
no. 33 (1969), p. 5-53.

The loss of much of their west African claim which arose from the El Pardo treaty of
1778 was a bitter disappointment for the Spanish. Río Muni's northern border was
fixed by German intransigence, but the enclave's eastern and southern boundaries
were delimited by a Franco-Spanish boundary commission in 1901. Agreement was
reached after sixteen years of difficult negotiation and a survey. In the end Spain
received only 26,000 square miles of her 800,000 square mile claim. This article
examines the drawing of Gabon's borders in general, noting that the section shared
with Río Muni was the most difficult.

216 **The report of the parliamentary delegation to Fernando Po and Río Muni – 1957**
Nigerian Government. Lagos: Federal Government Printers, 1957. 28p.
A brief but important summary of relations between Spanish Guinea and Nigeria on the eve of the latter's independence. Of particular significance are items on labour migration and related issues.

217 **International rivalry in the Bights of Benin and Biafra 1815-1885.**
W. H. Scotter. Unpublished thesis, University of London, 1933.
Scotter's history thesis provides a good overall look at the ranges, scopes and conflicts of British, French, German, Spanish and Portuguese influences in the Gulf of Guinea up to the Berlin Conference of 1885 which fixed all claims in the area.

218 **Special committee on the situation with regards to the implementation of the declaration on the colonial countries and peoples: Fernando Po, Ifni, Río Muni and the Spanish Sahara.**
United Nations Secretariat. New York: United Nations, 1964. 16p. (Document UN/A./A.C. 109/L. 144).
This working paper on decolonization calls on Spain to free her African dependencies. It should be noted that Fernando Po and Río Muni are dealt with as separate colonies, a distinction which would not be made by the UN four years later when Bubi leaders express their concerns about Equatorial Guinean independence.

Report of the International Commission of Inquiry into the existence of slavery and forced labor in the Republic of Liberia.
See item no. 93.

Les relations Gabon–Guinée Équatoriale: 1643-1977.
See item no. 224.

Equatorial Guinea–Nigerian relations: the diplomacy of labour.
See item no. 227.

Post-colonial

219 **South Africa seeks allies among island neighbours: foreign aid programme brings cattle and rumours to Equatorial Guinea.**
J. Brooke. *International Herald Tribune* (Paris), 22 Oct. 1987, p. 4.
In an attempt to break out of its isolation in the late 1980s, South Africa courted the Obiang régime with aid. This short article describes the situation.

220 **España y Francia pugnan por Guinea Ecuatorial.** (Spain and France struggle for Equatorial Guinea.)
Ignacio Cembrero. *El País* (Madrid), 23 April 1983, p. 1-2.
In the post-Macías era, Spain and France have competed for influence in Malabo. The latter has proved more successful. This article provides a representative Spanish view of the situation.

221 **Scénario pour un petit Biafra.** (A scenario for a little Biafra.)
Siradiou Diallo. *Jeune Afrique*, no. 617 (4 Nov. 1972), p. 22-5.
This French magazine article provides much information of Equatorial Guinean–Gabonese relations and the politics of petroleum in the area.

222 **The making of an African legend: the Biafra story.**
Frederick Forsyth.   London: Penguin, 1977. 286p.
As a Reuter's and BBC correspondent covering the Biafran side during the Nigerian civil war, Forsyth briefly relates the problems between the Red Cross and the Macías régime over the relief flights from Fernando Po into Biafra. His experiences with the Equatorial Guinean government at that time undoubtedly led to his involvement in a plot to overthrow Macías in 1972-73 which in turn led to Forsyth's *The Dogs of War*, a thinly disguised rewriting of this attempt.

223 **Communist powers and sub-Saharan Africa.**
Edited by Thomas H. Henriksen.   Stanford: Hoover Institution Press, 1981. 137p. bibliog.
This overview of relations between the Soviet bloc and black Africa before *glasnost* includes some material on Equatorial Guinea. Especially interesting are the comments on Soviet fishing in Equatorial Guinean waters during the Macías era (p. 14) and the expulsion of personnel from the Soviet Union and other communist powers after the 1979 coup.

224 **Les relations Gabon–Guinée Équatoriale: 1643-1977.**
(Gabonese–Equatorial Guinean relations: 1643-1977.)
Max Liniger-Goumaz.   In: *Africana: L'Afrique d'hier à demain*,
Geneva: Editions du Temps, 1977, p. 77-93.
Whether in the area of trade, border delimitation, smuggling or refugee settlement, relations between Equatorial Guinea and Gabon have been fraught with difficulties. This article surveys some of these issues and concentrates on Macías' attempts to sell some small islands in the Muni estuary and a sliver of Río Muni's eastern border territory to the Gabonese in the mid-1970s.

225 **Les relations entre le Gabon et la Guinée Equatoriale du temps de Macías Nguema.** (Relations between Gabon and Equatorial Guinea in the time of Macías Nguema.)
Agathe Manomba-Boukinda. Unpublished thesis, Université de Sorbonne, Paris, 1984.

This thesis provides an overview of Equatorial Guinean-Gabonese relations between 1968 and 1979. Among the topics detailed are border disputes, refugee and exile issues, trade and diplomacy.

226 **Equatorial Guinea: Mr. Botha's long hand.**
E. Momoh. *West Africa* (London), 30 Nov. 1987, p. 2335-6.

Momoh offers a good account of South Africa's attempts to influence the Obiang régime in the late 1980s.

227 **Equatorial Guinea–Nigerian relations: the diplomacy of labour.**
Akinjide Osuntokun.   Ibadan: Oxford University Press, 1978. 60p.

As senior lecturer in history at the University of Lagos, Osuntokun offers a concise and readable summary of Equatorial Guinean–Nigerian relations, both colonial and post-colonial. As would be expected, he concentrates on the labour issues which have been so controversial throughout this century. This monograph was supported by the Nigerian Institute of International Affairs.

Equatorial Guinea: an African tragedy.
See item no. 63.

Guinea: materia reservada. (Guinea: reserved material.)
See item no. 81.

La voz del pueblo. (The voice of the people.)
See item no. 168.

La voz del pueblo: suplemento. (The voice of the people: supplement.)
See item no. 169.

La voz del pueblo: suplemento no. 3. (The voice of the people: supplement 3.)
See item no. 170.

Equatorial Guinea – Macías country: the forgotten refugees.
See item no. 174.

Equatorial Guinea: the forgotten dictatorship.
See item no. 199.

African boundaries: a legal and diplomatic encyclopedia.
See item no. 214.

Nigerian exodus.
See item no. 269.

The Economy and Economic Development

Colonial

228 **Presente y futuro de la economía de Guinea.** (The Guinean economy: present and future.)
Juan Maria Bonelli y Rubio.   Barcelona, Spain: Casa de Guinea, 1945.

This report was given to a conference on Spanish Guinea by one of the colony's most progressive-minded governors-general. Forced to resign as a result of the 1947 teachers' pay dispute, Bonelli y Rubio seems to have taken a genuine concern for the welfare of the Spanish colony, in spite of his business connections with the colony and his almost stereotypical background as a colonial official.

229 **La evolución económica de Guinea Ecuatorial desde 1850 a 1968.** (The economic evolution of Equatorial Guinea from 1850 to 1968.)
Raphael Evita.   Unpublished thesis, Howard University, Washington DC, 1970. 206p.

Professor Evita offers a most impressive discussion of the development of the Equatorial Guinean economy. Unfortunately his work is largely eclipsed by the more recent thesis of Valentin Oyono Sa Abegue (see item no. 230).

The Economy and Economic Development. Colonial

230 L'évolution des structures productives et sociales de l'économie de la
Guinée Equatoriale 1858-1968. (The evolution of the productive and
social structures of the economy of Equatorial Guinea 1858-1968.)
Valentin Oyono Sa Abegue. Unpublished thesis, Université de Lyon
II, Lyon, 1985. 983p.
This important and highly regarded scholarly work traces the development of agrarian
capitalism and Spanish paternalism in Equatorial Guinea during the period of Spanish
colonialism. Also worthy of note are Oyono's descriptions of the religious and social
institutions developed by the Spanish and the Catholic Church.

Fernando Póo y el Muni, sus misterios, sus riquezas, su colonialización.
(Fernando Po and the Muni: their mysteries, their riches, their colonization.)
See item no. 13.

Notas geográficas, físicas y económicas sobre los territorios españoles del Golfo
de Guinea. (Geographical, physical and economic notes on the Spanish
territories in the Gulf of Guinea.)
See item no. 31.

De colonización y economía en la Guinea española. (Concerning colonization
and economics in Spanish Guinea.)
See item no. 77.

Equatorial Guinea: colonialism, state terror and the search for stability.
See item no. 175.

Avance del informe sobre somera explotación de posibilidades industriales.
(Advance report on summary exploitation of industrial possibilities.)
See item no. 250.

El bosque de la Guinea: exploración y explotación. (The forests of Guinea:
exploration and exploitation.)
See item no. 262.

Estudio sobre la constitución y explotación del bosque en la Guinea
Continental Española. (A study of the constitution and exploitation of the
forests of continental Spanish Guinea.)
See item no. 263.

La Guinée équatoriale, un pays méconnu. (Equatorial Guinea: the misunderstood land.)
See item no. 333.

Post-colonial

231 **Congo, Gabon, Equatorial Guinea: country report, analyses of economic and political trends.**
London: Economist Intelligence Unit. quarterly.

232 **Gabon, Equatorial Guinea: country profile, annual survey of political and economic background.**
London: Economist Intelligence Unit. annual.

233 **Quarterly review of Gabon, Congo, Cameroon, the Central African Republic, Chad and Equatorial Guinea.**
London: Economist Intelligence Unit. quarterly.

These three specialized publications of *The Economist* (items 231, 232 and 233) offer up-to-date economic, financial and political information for business. Accompanied by careful analysis and numerous statistics, they record and predict possible trends in Equatorial Guinea.

234 **The banking system of Gabon and the Central Bank of Equatorial Africa and Cameroon.**
Lorenzo Frediani.   Milan, Italy: Casse di Risparmio della Provincie Lombarde, 1974. 343p.

This work on the central African portion of the franc zone is relevant to Equatorial Guinea as background to the country's 1985 entry into the francophone Central African Economic and Customs Union.

235 **The economy of the Republic of Equatorial Guinea: recent evolution and prospects.**
International Bank for Reconstruction and Development.
Washington: International Development Agency, 27 Nov. 1972.

This World Bank document reflects concern over the economic consequences of the politics and policies of Equatorial Guinea's immediate post-independence period.

236 **Annual report.**
Washington: International Bank for Reconstruction and Development.
annual.

The World Bank's annual reviews provide general economic information and statistics for all member nations. The 1987 edition is of particular importance for Equatorial Guinean data.

237   **La République de Guinée Equatoriale: ses resources potentielles et virtuelles et possibilités de développement.** (The Republic of Equatorial Guinea: its potential resources and development possibilities.)
Armin Eric Kobel.   Unpublished thesis, University of Neuchâtel, Switzerland, 1976. 623p.

Kobel presents much economic analysis, geographical information and many statistical references in this scholarly work. This frequently cited thesis is the source of much information on and analysis of Equatorial Guinea's capabilities.

238   **Guinée Equatoriale: dossier d'information économique.** (Equatorial Guinea: economic information dossier.)
Paris: Ministère de la Coopération, June 1980. 100p.

This collection of economic information and statistics was compiled by the French to access the country's foreign aid requirements. As time would show such assistance would encourage closer Equatorial Guinea–French relations and Equatorial Guinean entry into the franc zone with five years.

239   **UNCTAD/UNDP project on training and advisory services on the GSP.**
New York: United Nations Development Programme, 27 March 1973. (Document INT-27).

The evacuation of Spanish citizens from Equatorial Guinea in 1969 left the country short of professional and technical personnel. This document describes the personnel assistance co-ordinated by the UN on behalf of Equatorial Guinea.

240   **UNDP country programme of the government of Equatorial Guinea.**
New York: United Nations Development Programme, 13 Sept. 1974. (Document DP/GC/EQG/R.1./RECOMMENDATION).

During the Macías era, the United Nations Development Programme set up a comprehensive plan for the country's revitalization and development. Due to government obstruction, corruption and the effects of human rights abuses, none of the projects sponsored by the UNDP succeeded, in spite of numerous attempts and silence on the subject of human rights on the part of the agencies involved.

241   **UNDP assistance requested by the government of Equatorial Guinea for the period of 1974-1978.**
New York: United Nations Development Programme, 23 Oct. 1974. (Document DP/GC/EQG/R.1).

This addition to item no. 240 lists the specific requests for aid presented to the UN by the Macías régime.

242 **Special economic assistance and disaster relief aid: assistance to Equatorial Guinea.**
United Nations Secretary General.   New York: United Nations, 19 August 1985. 27p. (Document A/40/430).

In responding to the desperate economic conditions which resulted from Macías' eleven year's of misrule and Obiang's inability to change the situation afterwards, the UN put together a special package of aid to overcome the country's immediate and most severe problems. This document provides the details of this programme.

Small is not beautiful: the story of Equatorial Guinea.
See item no. 1.

Tropical gangsters.
See item no. 23.

Equatorial Guinea: annual review 1984.
See item no. 38.

Equatorial Guinea – Macías country: the forgotten refugees.
See item no. 174.

Equatorial Guinea: colonialism, state terror and the search for stability.
See item no. 175.

Equatorial Guinea: the forgotten dictatorship.
See item no. 199.

Equatorial Guinea: machinations in founding a national bank.
See item no. 244.

Survey of African economies.
See item no. 245.

Etudes et statistiques de la BEAC. (Studies and statistics of the Bank of Central African States.)
See item no. 270.

La Guinée équatoriale, un pays méconnu. (Equatorial Guinea: the misunderstood land.)
See item no. 333.

Equatorial Guinea.
See item no. 334.

Finance and Banking

243 **La situation économique, monétaire et financière de la Guinée**
Equatoriale à la veille de son adhésion à la zone BEAC. (The economic,
monetary and financial situations of Equatorial Guinea on the eve of its
joining the BEAC zone.)
Etudes et Statistiques (Banque des Etats de l'Afrique Centrale,
Libreville), Jan. 1985, p. 17-32.
This important issue of the BEAC's quarterly discusses the state of Equatorial
Guinea's economy in the mid-1980s.

244 **Equatorial Guinea: machinations in founding a national bank.**
Robert C. Gard. *Munger Africana Library Notes* (California Institute
of Technology, Pasadena), Issue 27 (Oct. 1974). 46p.
The establishment of Equatorial Guinea's financial system was rife with corruption,
political influence and fraud. Gard examines the historical, political and economic
issues at work in the early years of independent Equatorial Guinea's financial
institutions.

245 **Survey of African economies.**
Washington: International Monetary Fund, 1973.
Financial information on newly independent Equatorial Guinea appears in vol. V,
Chapter 7 of this annual IMF study. Pages 314 to 454 analyse what was left after less
than three years of independence.

246 **Guinée Equatoriale et zone franc: réflexions sur un système monétaire et une récupération.** (Equatorial Guinea and the franc zone: reflections on a monetary system and a recovery.)
Max Liniger-Goumaz. *Genève-Afrique* (Geneva), vol. XXIII, no. 2 (1985), p. 137-46.
This is a critical look at the prospects and possibilities for Equatorial Guinea as part of the franc zone, which the country joined on 1 January 1985.

Small is not beautiful: the story of Equatorial Guinea.
See item no. 1.

Tropical gangsters.
See item no. 23.

Guinée Equatoriale: dossier d'information économique. (Equatorial Guinea: economic information dossier.)
See item no. 238.

Etudes et statistiques de la BEAC. (Studies and statistics of the Bank of Central African States.)
See item no. 270.

Equatorial Guinea.
See item no. 334.

Trade

247 **Yankee traders, old coasters and African middlemen.**
   G. E. Brooks, Jr.   Boston, Massachusetts: Boston University Press,
   1970. 370p. maps. bibliog.
This book, which deals mainly with American trade with west Africa, provides both
the background to and numerous details of 19th-century commerce in the Gulf of
Guinea. Illustrations are included.

248 **Report on figures of foreign trade of Spanish Guinea.**
   E. Soria Medina.   *US Joint Publications Research Service Translations
   on Africa* (Washington), no. 471 (16 Dec. 1966), p. 19-22.
Translations of Spanish data on trade since the Second World War.

Small is not beautiful: the story of Equatorial Guinea.
See item no. 1.

Travels in West Africa: Congo Français, Corisco and Cameroons.
See item no. 20.

Equatorial Guinea: colonialism, state terror and the search for stability.
See item no. 175.

Guinée Équatoriale: dossier d'information économique. (Equatorial Guinea:
economic information dossier.)
See item no. 238.

John Holt: a British merchant in West Africa in the era of imperialism.
See item no. 323.

Equatorial Guinea.
See item no. 334.

Industry

249 **Excelente calidad del petróleo de Guinea Ecuatorial, según los estudios de la empresa mixta Gepsa.** (The excellent quality of Equatorial Guinean petroleum, according to the studies of the mixed enterprise GEPSA.)
Rafael Fraguas. *El País* (Madrid), 28 April 1982, p. 65. map.
A brief and optimistic magazine report on oil exploration in the Gulf of Guinea north of Fernando Po. A map of oil deposits is included.

250 **Avance del informe sobre somera explotación de posibilidades industriales.** (Advance report on summary exploitation of industrial possibilities.)
Madrid: Instituto de Estudios Africanos, 1963. 75p.
A collection of short essays on the industrial potential of Equatorial Guinea, including food industries by R. Campos Nordmann (p. 34-40); paper, cellulose, yucca and wood derivatives by E. Carcamo Bredal (p. 46-63); carpentry, bottling and chemical industries by C. Laorden Jiménez (p. 44-5); and mines and minerals by J. Lizaur y Roldán (p. 32-3).

251 **The production of palm oil and soap.**
UNIDO/UNDP. Vienna: United Nations Industrial Development Organization, 1974. (Document SIS/EQU/71/801).
A short report on this once-thriving industry by R. van Tilt. Possibilities for development are included.

Small is not beautiful: the story of Equatorial Guinea.
See item no. 1.

Industry

Informe al gobierno de la República de Guinea Ecuatorial referente a política minera y petrolera. (A report to the government of the Republic of Equatorial Guinea relating to mineral and petroleum policy.)
See item no. 36.

Equatorial Guinea: annual review 1984.
See item no. 38.

Equatorial Guinea: the forgotten dictatorship.
See item no. 199.

Agriculture

252 Perspectivas de la explotación del aceite de palma en la Guinea española.
(Perspectives on palm oil exploitation in Spanish Guinea.)
E. Fickendey. *Archivos del Instituto de Estudios Africanos* (Madrid),
nos 28, 29 (March, June 1954), p. 23-33, 25-30.
An authoritative two-article series on palm oil production in the colonial era.

253 Livestock breeding in Equatorial Guinea.
Rome: Food and Agriculture Organization, 1970.
An optimistic report on the past, present and future of livestock breeding in Equatorial
Guinea by two FAO experts, Caldwell and Brouwer.

254 Agricultura de los territorios españoles del Golfo de Guinea.
(Agriculture in the Spanish territories of the Gulf of Guinea.)
Madrid: Instituto de Estudios Africanos, 1948.
A survey of plantation agriculture in colonial Spanish Guinea, concentrating on cacao
on Fernando Po and coffee and oil palm in Rio Muni.

255 Quarterly bulletin of cocoa statistics.
London: International Cocoa Organization. quarterly.
As Equatorial Guinea's chief export has traditionally been cacao and cocoa products,
this periodical offers numerous figures on production and trade. The September 1985
issue is particularly good.

256 **Clasificación y características de los cacaos de Fernando Póo.**
(Classification and characteristics of the cacaos of Fernando Po.)
Jaime Nosti Nava, J. Alvarez Aparaicio.   Madrid: Dirección General
de Marruecos y Colonias, 1943. 73p.

Fourth in a series of agricultural monographs sponsored by the Dirección de
Agricultura de los Territorios Españoles del Golfo de Guinea, this handbook provides
a comprehensive survey of all types of cacao cultivation on Fernando Po.

257 **Agricultura de Guinea, promesa para España.** (Agriculture in Guinea,
promise for Spain.)
Jaime Nosti Nava.   Madrid: Instituto de Estudios Africanos, 1948.
90p.

This tract with a number of illustrations is Nosti Nava's observations on what the
future of Equatorial Guinean agriculture could hold, particularly in terms of profits for
Spain.

258 **Cómo es y cómo se poda el cafeto 'Liberia'.** (How and why to prune the
'Liberia' coffee tree.)
Jaime Nosti Nava, F. Jimenez Cuende.   Madrid: Instituto de Estudios
Africanos, 1949. 105p.

Nosti Nava and Jimenez go far beyond the mere technical details described by the title
of this work and relate the benefits which increased coffee cultivation could bring
Spanish Guinea.

259 **La agricultura en Guinea Española.** (Agriculture in Spanish Guinea.)
Jaime Nosti Nava.   Madrid: Instituto de Estudios Africanos, 1955.
376p. bibliog.

This is a classic work on agriculture in Equatorial Guinea in which Nosti Nava draws
on his extensive experience and past publications to provide an excellent overview.

260 **Cocoa production: economic and botanical perspectives.**
Edited by John Simmons.   New York: Praeger, 1976. 413p.

A collection of essays and lectures on the economics and development of cocoa
production and trade in Latin America and west Africa, including Equatorial Guinea.

261 **Cocoa.**
G. A. R. Wood, R. A. Lass.   London: Longman, 1985. 620p. bibliog.

This work is the chief reference in English on cacao cultivation and cocoa production.
As Equatorial Guinea was a major producer of cacao and continues to be dependent
on cocoa as an export, it is an indispensable reference for understanding the country.

Small is not beautiful: the story of Equatorial Guinea.
See item no. 1.

Equatorial Guinea: an African tragedy.
See item no. 63.

Equatorial Guinea – Macías country: the forgotten refugees.
See item no. 174.

Equatorial Guinea: the forgotten dictatorship.
See item no. 199.

Forestry

262 **El bosque de la Guinea: exploración y explotación.** (The forests of
Guinea: exploration and exploitation.)
J. M. Capdevielle.   Madrid: Instituto de Estudios Africanos, 1947.
235p.
Equatorial Guinea is a source of a number of tropical woods. Of special interest is
okoumé which is excellently suited for making plywood. The Spanish, as illustrated by
this book, saw lumbering in Río Muni as a lucrative addition to cacao cultivation on
Fernando Po. Macías and Obiang would use timbering as an easier alternative to
cacao. Capdevielle describes the forests and the early timber industry.

263 **Estudio sobre la constitución y explotación del bosque en la Guinea
Continental Española.** (A study of the constitution and exploitation of
the forests of continental Spanish Guinea.)
Pedro Fúster Riera.   Madrid: Diana Artes Gráficas, 1941. 132p.
This early study supported by the Dirección General de la Marruecos y Colonias (the
Spanish Colonial Office) describes the potential of Río Muni's forests.

264 **Primera contribución al conocimiento de las maderas de la Guinea
continental española.** (A preliminary contribution to the knowledge of
the wood of continental Spanish Guinea.)
Pedro Fúster Riera, L. Martín González.   Madrid: Instituto de
Estudios Africanos, 1953. 2 vols. 454p. bibliog.
This illustrated reference is the best guide to Río Muni's forests, colonial timber
industry and its various woods, their characteristics and products.

265   **Situation forestière en Guinée Equatoriale.** (The forestry situation in Equatorial Guinea.)
      B. Vannierre.   Rome: Food and Agriculture Organization, June-July 1969.

In an attempt to expand the Equatorial Guinean economy, the FAO published this report as a reference to industry, government and foreign aid donors.

Labour

Colonial

266 **Involuntary labour since the abolition of slavery: a survey of compulsory labour throughout the world.**
Willemina Kloosterboer.   Leiden, The Netherlands: E. J. Brill, 1960.
215p. bibliog.
Pages 167 and 168 of this general study by a Dutch author looks at Spanish Guinea.

267 **Labor conditions in Equatorial Guinea.**
Office of Foreign Labor and Trade.   Washington: US Dept. of State,
1966.
This report by the US government examines the labour situation in the country during the autonomy period when the number of Nigerian migrant workers on Fernando Po plantations was at its peak.

Travels in West Africa: Congo Français, Corisco and Cameroons.
See item no. 20.

Report of the International Commission of Inquiry into the existence of slavery and forced labor in the Republic of Liberia.
See item no. 93.

Equatorial Guinea – Macías country: the forgotten refugees.
See item no. 174.

Equatorial Guinea: the forgotten dictatorship.
See item no. 199.

**The report of the parliamentary delegation to Fernando Po and Río Muni –
1957.**
See item no. 216.

Equatorial Guinea–Nigerian relations: the diplomacy of labour.
See item no. 227.

Post-colonial

268 **The cocoa slaves of Fernando Po.**
Mark Arnold-Foster.   *The Guardian* (London), vol. 115, no. 21
(21 Nov. 1976), p. 68-9.
Following evacuation of Nigerian workers in 1976, Macías had between 20,000 and
25,000 Río Munians press-ganged for forced labour on the plantations of Fernando Po.
Concentrating on labour issues and the introduction of state slavery under Macías, this
article also alludes to the general economic and political conditions in the country.

269 **Nigerian exodus.**
Africa (London), no. 55 (March 1976), p. 57
This short but very informative article describes the violent 1976 evacuation of
Nigerian migrant workers on Fernando Po and the accompanying strain in
Nigerian–Equatorial Guinean relations.

Equatorial Guinea: an African tragedy.
See item no. 63.

Equatorial Guinea – Macías country: the forgotten refugees.
See item no. 174.

Equatorial Guinea: the forgotten dictatorship.
See item no. 199.

Equatorial Guinea–Nigerian relations: the diplomacy of labour.
See item no. 227.

Statistics

270 **Etudes et statistiques de la BEAC.** (Studies and statistics of the Bank of
   Central African States.)
   Libreville: Banque des Etats de l'Afrique Centrale. monthly.
Issues of the BEAC's monthly since January 1985 are important for Equatorial
Guinean financial and economic statistics.

271 **Statistics of Equatorial Guinea: data to explain a political disaster.**
   Max Liniger-Goumaz. Geneva: Editions du Temps, 1986.
Few reliable statistics have been forthcoming from Equatorial Guinea since
independence. Many officials responsible for statistical surveys were executed or
imprisoned by Macías, including the director of the Río Muni Statistical Office who
was shot in 1970 for refusing to declare that the country had a population of a million.
This situation has presented problems for scholars, businessmen, aid donors, banks
and governments alike. This analysis of statistics from and about the country seeks to
find some truths in the chaos which has surrounded the Macías and Obiang régimes.

Small is not beautiful: the story of Equatorial Guinea.
See item no. 1.

Equatorial Guinea – 1920 census.
See item no. 99.

**Congo, Gabon, Equatorial Guinea: country report, analyses of economic and
political trends.**
See item no. 231.

**Gabon, Equatorial Guinea: country profile, annual survey of political and
economic background.**
See item no. 232.

Quarterly review of Gabon, Congo, Cameroon, the Central African Republic, Chad and Equatorial Guinea.
See item no. 233.

La République de Guinée Equatoriale: ses resources potentielles et virtuelles et possibilités de développement. (The Republic of Equatorial Guinea: its potential resources and development possibilities.)
See item no. 237.

Guinée Equatoriale: dossier d'information économique. (Equatorial Guinea: economic information dossier.)
See item no. 238.

Report on figures of foreign trade of Spanish Guinea.
See item no. 248.

Spanish Guinea.
See item no. 328.

La Guinée équatoriale, un pays méconnu. (Equatorial Guinea: the misunderstood land.)
See item no. 333.

Equatorial Guinea.
See item no. 334.

The Environment and Climate

272   **Guía meteorológica de las provincias de Guinea.** (A meteorological
      guide for the province of Guinea.)
      Rafael Capuz Bonilla.   Madrid: Instituto de Estudios Africanos, 1961.
      65p. maps.
A brief guide to the climate of Spanish Guinea. Illustrations are included.

273   **Climatología de los territorios españoles del Golfo de Guinea.**
      (A climatology of the Spanish territories in the Gulf of Guinea.)
      Jaime Nosti Nava.   Madrid: Talleres Tipográficos Espasa-Calpe, 1942.
      67p.
This climatological study intended primarily as a reference work for agriculture is
second in a series of monographs sponsored by the Dirección de Agricultura de los
Territorios Españoles del Golfo de Guinea.

Calypso **explores an undersea canyon.**
See item no. 25.

**Projecto de investigación y conservación de la naturaleza en Guinea
Ecuatorial.** (A nature conservation and investigation project in Equatorial
Guinea.)
See item no. 46.

El bosque de la Guinea: exploración y explotación. (The forests of Guinea:
exploration and exploitation.)
See item no. 262.

Estudio sobre la constitución y explotación del bosque en la Guinea Continental Española. (A study on the constitution and exploitation of the forests of continental Spanish Guinea.)
See item no. 263.

Situation forestière en Guinée Equatoriale. (The forestry situation in Equatorial Guinea.)
See item no. 265.

Education

274 **El Patronato de Indígenas de Guinea: institución ejemplar.** (The
Patronato de Indígenas de Guinea: an exemplary institution.)
H. Altozano Moraleda. *Archivos des Instituto de Estudios Africanos*
(Madrid), no. 40 (March 1957), p. 49-63.

The semi-official Native Patronage Office was the institution which, more than anything else, controlled the lives of the Spanish colony's inhabitants. Tied to the Roman
Catholic Church, it ran the educational, health and welfare systems of the colony and
determined who would be considered legally 'assimilated' for tax, labour and voting
purposes. This article is a glowing and blinkered look at the 'Patronato' by a Spaniard.

275 **Enseñanza en la Guinea Española.** (Education in Spanish Guinea.)
R. H. Alvarez. *Archivos des Instituto de Estudios Africanos* (Madrid),
no. 22 (1951), p. 23-33.

Under the Spanish, primary education and some technical training was provided to
most of the population, but students wishing to pursue higher studies were required to
leave the country, as education beyond what was required by the administration,
plantations and lumber companies was neglected. Alvarez provides an overview of
primary and religious education in the colony.

276 **Equatorial Guinea: proposals for the reconstruction and development of
education.**
Paris; UNESCO, Sept. 1984. 144p. maps. (Document EFM 125).

Education is seen by the United Nations as a priority in the restoration of human rights
and reasonable living conditions. In order to accomplish these goals UNESCO
commissioned this report with statistical tables. However, the mismanagement of the
country under Obiang has caused progress in this and other areas to be hampered.

Small is not beautiful: the story of Equatorial Guinea.
See item no. 1.

Equatorial Guinea – Macías country: the forgotten refugees.
See item no. 174.

Equatorial Guinea: colonialism, state terror and the search for stability.
See item no. 175.

La Guinée équatoriale, un pays méconnu. (Equatorial Guinea: the misunderstood land.)
See item no. 333.

Literature

277 **Introduction to a Fang oral art genre: Gabon and Cameroon meet.**
Pierre Alexandre. *Bulletin of the School of Oriental and African
Studies* (London), vol. XXXVII, no. 1 (1974), p. 1-7.
A brief discussion of the ballad and poetic traditions on the Fang.

278 **Voces de espuma.** (Voices of foam.)
C. Bokesa. Malabo: Centro Cultural Hispano-Guineano, 1987.
One of a number of poetry collections sponsored by the Spanish-funded Centro
Cultural Hispano-Guineano in Malabo.

279 **Sueños en mi selva: antología poética.** (Dreams in my jungle: an
anthology of poetry.)
Juan Boneke Balboa. Malabo: Centro Cultural Hispano-Guineano,
1987.
A poetry anthology in Spanish.

280 **Wit and wisdom from West Africa.**
Richard F. Burton. New York: Negro University Press, 1969. 455p.
Described as 'a book of proverbial philosophy, idioms, enigmas and laconisms',
Burton's collection includes a number of Fang and Mpongwe proverbs and idiomatic
usages which reveal a bit of the philosophy, society and world-view of the region's
inhabitants.

281 **The dogs of war.**
Frederick Forsyth. London: Hutchinson, 1974. 408p.
As a result of his experiences in financing an unsuccessful attempt to oust the Macías
régime in 1972-73, Forsyth wrote this novel of a successful mercenary-led overthrow of
an African tyrant. His book is peopled with thinly disguised characters representing

Macías, Biafran general Ojukwu and real mercenaries. A United Artists film of the same title (produced by Larry de Waay and directed by John Irvin) was based on Forsyth's book and in some ways makes the characters and events even less disguised. See also item no. 85.

282 **Tierra negra.** (Black earth.)
D. Manfredi Cano. Barcelona, Spain: Luis de Caralt, 1957.
A novel by a Spaniard set in Spanish Guinea.

283 **Le Mvett.** (The Mvet.)
Tsira Ndong Ndoutoume. Paris: Présence Africaine, 1970. 157p.
A unique collection of Fang tales named after the guitar-like musical instrument favoured by the tribe.

284 **Antología de la literatura Ecuatoguineana.** (An anthology of Equato-Guinean literature.)
Donato Ndongo Bidiyogo. Madrid: Editora Nacional, 1985.
As director of Malabo's Centro Cultural Hispano-Guineano and a writer himself, Ndongo Bidiyogo edited this collection of literature from various parts of the country.

285 **Le Mvet: un genre littéraire Fang.** (The Mvet: a Fang literary genre.)
M. Nkoa ze Lecourt. Unpublished thesis, EPHE, Paris, 1973.
Popular among the Fang, the Mvet balladeers have religious and social (and more recently political) roles. This study in French examines their role and literary aspects in Gabon and southern Cameroon, as well as in Equatorial Guinea.

286 **Ekomo.**
Mária Nsué Angüe. Madrid: Universidad Nacional de Educación a Distancia, 1985. 194p.
A novel in Spanish about the Fang by a Fang. The author was the wife of José Nsué Angüe Osa, the Equatorial Guinean ambassador to Ethiopia who was poisoned by Macías' agents in late 1976.

287 **El baile de los malditos.** (The dance of the damned.)
Daniel Oyono Ayingono. Bata: Equatorial Guinean Government Press, 1974. 287p.
This booklet by a nephew of Macías provides a chilling fictionalized account of the trials which followed the June 1974 coup attempt. Its title is believed to be influenced by the name given to the nightly public tortures carried on at Blackbich Prison in Malabo during the time of Macías.

Equatorial Guinea: colonialism, state terror and the search for stability
See item no. 175.

Art, Music and Architecture

288 **Leandro Mbomio en la integración de la negritud.** (Leandro Mbomio in the integration of negritude.)
C. Arean. Madrid, 1975. 175p. bibliog.

The works and influences of Leandro Mbomio, a Fang sculptor of international repute (later Minister of Culture under Obiang), are described in this illustrated guide.

289 **Sculpture of Africa.**
W. Fagg (text), B. Quint (drawings). New York: Thames and Hudson, 1958. 256p. bibliog.

Prefaced by R. Linton, this illustrated survey of African sculpture includes examples of Fang sculpture on pages 160 and 164-77.

290 **Fang architectonics.**
James W. Fernandez. Philadelphia, Pennsylvania: Institute for the Study of Human Issues, 1977. 41p.

Accompanied by drawings and other illustrations, this is only major work on Fang architecture.

291 **Music from an equatorial microcosm: Fang Bwiti music (with MBiri selections).**
Recorded and annotated by James W. Fernandez. Folkways Records (New York) FE 4214.

A selection of Bwiti and MBiri (Bieri) music is presented on this recording.

292 **La música en la Guinea española.** (Music in Spanish Guinea.)
Carlos González Echegaray. *Archivos del Instituto de Estudios Africanos* (Madrid), no. 38 (June 1956), p. 19-30.
This article provides a short description of the musical traditions of the country.

293 **La música y el baile en los territorios españoles del Golfo de Guinea.**
(Music and dance in the Spanish territories of the Gulf of Guinea.)
R. Ibarrola Monasterio. *Africa* (Madrid), no. 142 (Oct. 1953), p. 15-17.
A brief and somewhat racist account of native culture in Spanish Guinea.

294 **Tipología de la cerámica de Fernando Po.** (A typology of the ceramics of Fernando Po.)
P. Martín. *La Guinea Español* (Santa Isabel), 1960. 36p.
A brief illustrated guide to the ceramics and pottery of Fernando Po.

Mass Media

The press

295 **Africa.**
Barcelona, Spain, June 1985- . monthly.
A somewhat leftist tabloid-size newsletter circulating among Equatorial Guineans and other Africans and Africanists in Europe. Currently edited by Foday Sadiku Fofanah.

296 **Africa.**
Madrid: Instituto de Estudios Africanos, Jan. 1947- . monthly.
This illustrated publication of the Instituto de Estudios Africanos has presented much good scholarly work on Equatorial Guinea in spite of frequently displayed colonialist biases.

297 **Africa 2000.**
Malabo: Centro Cultural Hispano-Guineano, 1987- . quarterly.
A cultural review published by the Centro Cultural Hispano-Guineano in Malabo.

298 **Africa Confidential.**
London: Miramoor Publications, 15 Jan. 1960- . fortnightly.
This fortnightly newsletter has published excellent research on the background and details behind African political news. Although material pertaining to Equatorial Guinea appears on average in only two or three issues a year, it is usually of a unique nature.

299   **Africa Report.**
New York: African-American Institute, July 1956- . monthly.
As the African-American Institute's magazine, this monthly has presented African affairs in a consistently readable manner since the first sub-Saharan nations gained their independence from European colonial powers. Issues which have appeared around important events in Equatorial Guinea (independence in 1968, the 1979 *coup d'état*, etc.) have contained numerous in-depth articles on the country.

300   **Ager.**
Santa Isabel: Servicio Agronómico de la Guinea Española, 1951-65. quarterly.
This publication contains agricultural news of the immediate pre-independence era.

301   **Amnesty Action.**
Washington, DC: Amnesty International. monthly.
As a watchdog of human rights, Amnesty International's monthly American newspaper presents news of the situation in Equatorial Guinea at least once a year. The British equivalent of this publication is *British Amnesty*, which has also featured news on the country.

302   **Boletín Agrícola de los territorios españoles del Golfo de Guinea.**
(Agricultural bulletin of the Spanish territories in the Gulf of Guinea.)
Santa Isabel: Cámera Oficial Agrícola, 1943-64.
The official agricultural journal of Spanish Guinea.

303   **Boletín Oficial de las provincias de Fernando Póo y Río Muni.** (Official bulletin of the provinces of Fernando Po and Río Muni.)
Santa Isabel: Fernando Po and Río Muni Provincial Governments, 1959-68. semi-monthly.
This official organ of the administration of Spanish Guinea during the era of 'provincialization' supersedes and continues the numbering of item no. 304.

304   **Boletín Oficial de los territorios españoles del Golfo de Guinea.** (Official bulletin of the Spanish territories in the Gulf of Guinea.)
Madrid: Dirección General de Marruecos y Colonias, March 1907-Sept. 1959. semi-monthly.
This official publication of the colonial administration (along with its successor, item no. 303) recorded laws, events and policies in the colonies throughout most of the 20th-century colonial period.

305   **Boletín.** (Bulletin.)
Santa Isabel: Cámara Agrícola Oficial de Fernando Póo, 1907-22. monthly.
An early news publication of the Fernando Po Official Agricultural Chamber, the association of planters.

306 **El Defensor de Guinea.** (The defender of Guinea.)
Santa Isabel, 1930-36. fortnightly.
A pre-Franco newspaper.

307 **Ebano.** (Ebony.)
Santa Isabel, 1939-41 and re-established in 1979.
Meant to be a daily newspaper, *Ebano*'s frequency has varied both in its colonial and present-day forms.

308 **La Guinea Española.** (Spanish Guinea.)
Santa Isabel: Misioneros Hijos del Immaculado Corazón de María, 1907-68.
The longest-running publication in Spanish Guinea, *La Guinea Española* contained news and much material on local life, including local stories and legends. In spite of its Catholic and colonialist biases, it presented much of value.

309 **La Hoja del Lunes.** (The Monday page.)
Santa Isabel, 1968-72. weekly.
This newspaper deteriorated into a propaganda sheet under Macías.

310 **Index on Censorship.**
London: PEN International. monthly.
PEN International is a human rights organization for writers and journalists. This is their monthly magazine which frequently contains news about censorship and other human rights violations in Equatorial Guinea.

311 **La Libertad.** (Liberty.)
Bata: Prensa La Libertad, 1968-69. weekly.
This newspaper, which was closed by Macías after the 1969 coup attempt, superseded item no. 313.

312 **El Nacionalista.** (The Nationalist.)
Santa Isabel: Falangist Party of Spanish Guinea, 1937-39. fortnightly.
The colony's first Falangist newspaper.

313 **Poto-Poto.**
Bata, 1951-67 and re-established in the 1980s. monthly.
Originally published by the Patronato de Indígenas during the colonial era, this has been Bata's only newspaper and one of a very few newspapers anywhere in Fang. Circulation is currently quite irregular. Since 1985 it has been published by the Equatorial Guinean government.

314 **Revista de la Diputación Provincial.** (The Provincial Assembly review.)
Santa Isabel: Fernando Po Provincial Government, 1961-64.
The official organ of Fernando Po's legislature during the period of 'provincialization'.

315 **West Africa.**
London: West Africa Publishing Co., 1917- . weekly.
One of a few English-language publications which has regular news items on
Equatorial Guinea.

Equatorial Guinea.
See item no. 334.

Press freedom

316 **Les rapports d'Amnesty International et la désinformation.**
Max Liniger-Goumaz. *Genève-Afrique* (Geneva), vol. XXIV, no. 2
(Dec. 1986), p. 137-46.
Citing the Obiang government's press restrictions and attempts to circulate disinforma-
tion, Professor Liniger-Goumaz disputes press statements that post-Macías Equatorial
Guinea is becoming a 'paradise of human rights'.

Small is not beautiful: the story of Equatorial Guinea.
See item no. 1.

Guinea: materia reservada. (Guinea: reserved material.)
See item no. 81.

La voz del pueblo. (The voice of the people.)
See item no. 168.

Equatorial Guinea – Macías country: the forgotten refugees.
See item no. 174.

Interview with Macías.
See item no. 324.

Biographies

317 **Richard F. Burton.**
Glenn S. Burne.   Boston: Twayne, 1985. 168p. (Twayne's English
Authors Series).
This biography of Burton, who was Consul to the Bights of Biafra and Benin from
1861 to 1864, examines him as a scholar and explorer, as well as an author.

318 **Iradier**
José Cordero Torres.   Madrid: Instituto de Estudios Políticos, 1944.
213p. maps.
This biography of Manuel Iradier glorifies the explorer as a hero, the official view of
the Franco régime. Nevertheless, it provides a good deal of factual background and
personal details. Illustrations are included.

319 **Mary Kingsley: a reassessment.**
John Flint.   *Journal of African History*, vol. IV, no. 1 (1963), p. 95-
104.
This article seeks to dispel some of the distortions of earlier romanticized accounts of
Kingsley's life.

320 **A voyager out.**
Katherine Frank.   New York: Ballantine, 1986. 333p. bibliog.
Parts two and three of this well-written biography of Mary Kingsley include much
material on Mary's research on Fernando Po, among the Bubis, in Fang territories and
on Corisco. Frequent references are also made to other personalities significant in the
development of what would become Equatorial Guinea, particularly John Holt and
Robert H. Nassau. Photos, including some taken by Kingsley herself, are included.

321 **Toda la verdad: mi intervención en Guinea.** (All the truth: my
intervention in Guinea.)
José Antonio García Trevijano.   Barcelona, Spain: Ediciones Dronte
1977. 151p.

As mentor and supporter of Macías, Spanish law professor García Trevijano bears a
good deal of responsibility for the Equatorial Guinean tyrant's reign of terror. García
ran Macías' 1968 presidential election campaign, financed his propaganda, wrote many
of the dictator's speeches (and perhaps even laws) and made several attempts to
develop the country after independence. As a result of his political and financial
dealings with the Macías régime, García's passport was revoked and his political career
in the Spanish Socialist Workers' Party was ended in scandal. This book is his
description of and justifications for his actions.

322 **Macías y yo.** (Macías and I.)
José Antonio García Trevijano.   *Informaciones* (Madrid), 23 Aug.
1979. 4p.

This short article continues García Trevijano's memoirs of his connections with the
Equatorial Guinean dictator. See also item no. 321.

323 **John Holt: a British merchant in West Africa in the era of imperialism.**
Cherry Gertzel.   Unpublished thesis, Nuffield College, Oxford, 1959.

This unpublished doctoral thesis provides good biographical sketch of John Holt whose
company was of prime importance in opening the western equatorial coasts of Africa
to trade.

324 **Interview with Macías.**
Graham Mytton.   BBC Monitor Report SWB ME/5111/B/1 of Lagos
Radio (15:30 GMT, 17 Jan. 1976).

On 30 July 1975, while covering the Kampala OAU summit, BBC reporter Graham
Mytton had a lengthy interview with Macías in which the Equatorial Guinean dictator
denied that human rights abuses were going on in his country. Clearly hostile to the
press, Macías rambled on, often incoherently, about Spanish colonialism and the many
conspiracies he believed were working against him. This interview, segments of which
are reprinted in items 63 and 199, offers a rare look at the personality of Macías.

325 **Captain Sir Richard Francis Burton.**
Edward Rice.   New York: Scribners, 1990. 669p. bibliog.

This lengthy and well-written recent biography of Burton includes material (Chapter 24
– Santa Isabel) on his stay in and travels from Fernando Po while consul there.

326 **Victorian women travel writers in Africa.**
Catherine B. Stevenson.   Boston: Twayne, 1982. 184p. bibliog.

Stevenson's examination of 19th-century British women travel-writers concentrates
heavily on Lady Florence Douglas Dixie and Mary Henrietta Kingsley, the latter
having travelled widely in the lands around the Gulf of Guinea.

Biographies

327 **Robert Hamill Nassau 1835-1921: Presbyterian pioneer missionary to equatorial west Africa.**
Raymond W. Teuwissen.   Unpublished thesis, Louisville Theological Seminary, Louisville, Kentucky, 1973.
The amazing life and works of Presbyterian missionary Nassau are recorded in this biographical thesis, which complements Nassau's own writings well.

Equatorial Guinea: an African tragedy.
See item no. 63.

Equatorial Guinea – Macías country: the forgotten refugees.
See item no. 174.

Psychoses of power: African personal dictatorships.
See item no. 181.

Personal rule in black Africa.
See item no. 183.

Autopsy of a miracle.
See item no. 187.

The trial of Macías in Equatorial Guinea – the story of a dictatorship.
See item no. 190.

A historical dictionary of Equatorial Guinea.
See item no. 332.

La Guinée équatoriale, un pays méconnu. (Equatorial Guinea: the misunderstood land.)
See item no. 333.

Reference Works

328 Spanish Guinea.
Historical Section of the Foreign Office.   In: *Spanish and Italian African Possessions and Independent States*. London: HMSO, 1920. vol. XX, no. 125. 60p. bibliog.

This handbook, prepared by the British Foreign Office and also reprinted in 1969 by Greenwood Press of New York, offers a comprehensive review of post-First World War Fernando Po, Río Muni and Annobón. Chapters include information, facts and statistics on physical and political geography, political history, social and political conditions and economic conditions. Appendices provide extracts from the Treaties of San Ildefonso (1777), El Pardo (1778) and the Franco-Spanish Convention of 1900; and pre-World War I foreign trade statistics.

329 Keesing's contemporary archives.
London: Longman, 1954- . monthly

Keesing's researchers compile regular records of political, diplomatic and economic events throughout the world. These compilations, which provide an excellent base for research, are gleaned from several hundred sources in the world press and provide an ongoing archive of significant events, personalities in power, cabinet compositions, election results and other facts and figures for all countries. Renamed *Keesing's Record of World Events* after 1988, its coverage of Equatorial Guinea has been exceptionally good but items of news have often been delayed for considerable amounts of time. Nevertheless, in many ways Keesing's has presented and continues to present the most comprehensive, accurate and objective account in English of events in Equatorial Guinea.

330 Africa contemporary record.
Edited by Colin Legum.   London: Rex Collings. annual.

The Equatorial Guinea entries of this voluminous annual (1969 to the present) provide a continuous record of events, personalities, policies and issues of the country.

331 **Africa research bulletin.**
Exeter: Africa Research Ltd, Jan. 1964- . monthly.
This research publication is divided into two sections: Series A. political, social and
cultural; and Series B. economic, financial and technical. Over the years a good deal of
material on Equatorial Guinea has been regularly reported and analysed by this
monthly publication.

332 **A historical dictionary of Equatorial Guinea.**
Max Liniger-Goumaz.   Metuchen, New Jersey: Scarecrow, 1979,
revised and expanded 1988. 238p. bibliog.
This reference work on Equatorial Guinea is useful as it contains much information not
found elsewhere in English, but due to its format it hardly displays the careful
scholarship of Liniger-Goumaz's other work (item no. 333 is a similar but superior
reference in French). Although described as an historical dictionary, this book also
contains a large amount of geographical, biographical, economic and social data, and
its bibliography is one of the largest in English.

333 **La Guinée équatoriale, un pays méconnu.** (Equatorial Guinea: the
misunderstood land.)
Max Liniger-Goumaz.   Paris: L'Harmattan, 1979. 512p. maps. bibliog.
This French-language single-volume encyclopaedia by the most noted expert on
Equatorial Guinea is the best reference available on the history, politics, economy,
society and international relations of that country. Many statistics and much
biographical material not available elsewhere are presented in Professor Liniger-
Goumaz's remarkable work.

334 **Equatorial Guinea.**
René Pélissier.   In: *Africa South of the Sahara*, London: Europa
Publications. annual since 1968. bibliog.
Entries in this authoritative annual are divided into a number of sections beginning
with essays on physical and social geography, recent history and the economy. These
sections are written by a leading expert on the particular country covered, and in the
case of Equatorial Guinea the author is René Pélissier. Following these background
pieces are a survey of area, population, economic, transport and education statistics
and a directory which describes the country's constitution, government, legislature,
political organizations, diplomatic representation, courts, religious institution, the mass
media, finance, trade and industry and transport. This information is accompanied by
appropriate names and addresses. Each entry ends with a short bibliography.

Small is not beautiful: the story of Equatorial Guinea.
See item no. 1.

Equatorial Guinea: an African tragedy.
See item no. 63.

A dictionary of black African civilization.
See item no. 103.

Political handbook of the world.
See item no. 191.

African boundaries: a legal and diplomatic encyclopedia.
See item no. 214.

Congo, Gabon, Equatorial Guinea: country report, analyses of economic and political trends.
See item no. 231.

Gabon, Equatorial Guinea: country profile, annual survey of political and economic background.
See item no. 232.

Quarterly review of Gabon, Congo, Cameroon, the Central African Republic, Chad and Equatorial Guinea.
See item no. 233.

Guinea Ecuatorial: bibliografía general.
See items no. 337 and 338.

Bibliographies

335 Spanish Guinea: an annotated bibliography.
Sanford Berman. Unpublished thesis, Catholic University of
America, Washington DC, 1961 597p.

As the first major bibliographical work on Equatorial Guinea, Berman's thesis
provides some 600 well-annotated book and article entries.

336 Materials on west African history in French archives.
Patricia Carson. London: Athlone Press, 1963. 170p.

This bibliography of French sources contains numerous entries on western equatorial
Africa, including Spanish Guinea.

337 Guinea Ecuatorial: bibliografía general. (Equatorial Guinea: general
bibliography.)
Max Liniger-Goumaz. Bern: Commission Nationale Suisse pour
l'UNESCO, 1976. vols and I and II.

Under the auspices of the Swiss National Commission for UNESCO, Max Liniger-
Goumaz began this general bibliography for Equatorial Guinea. See item no. 338.

338 Guinea Ecuatorial: bibliografía general. (Equatorial Guinea: general
bibliography.)
Max Liniger-Goumaz. Geneva: Editions du Temps, 1978-87. vols III,
IV, V and VI.

Building on the above entry, Liniger-Goumaz has completed an additional four
volumes with a Geneva publisher, making his *Guinea Ecuatorial: bibliografía general*
the single most important research tool on Equatorial Guinea. Totalling some 11,300
references, this series is valuable not only for studies of Equatorial Guinea but also for
adjacent countries.

339   **Spanish-speaking Africa: a guide to official publications.**
Susan Knoke Rishworth.   Washington, DC: Library of Congress,
1973. 66p.

This excellent bibliographical reference deals solely with official or officially sponsored
publications and articles. They are principally from the colonial era but there are also a
few from the immediate post-independence period.

Index

The index is a single alphabetical sequence of authors (personal and corporate), titles of publications, place-names and subjects. Index entries refer both to the main items and to other works mentioned in the notes to each item. Title entries are in italics. Numeration refers to the items as numbered.

Map of Equatorial Guinea

This map shows the more important towns and other features.

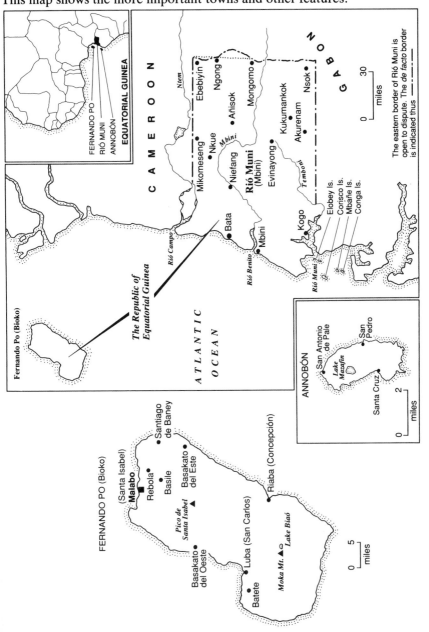